I Met More Ghosts

At Gettysburg

A Journalist's Paranormal Journey Continues

Ordering Information

Additional copies of *I Met More Ghosts at Gettysburg: A Journalist's Paranormal Journey Continues,* may be purchased for $16.95, plus $4 shipping and handling, from Faded Banner Publications, P.O. Box 101, Bryan, OH 43506, telephone 1-888-799-3787 (toll free), or on the Web at www.fadedbanner.com. Dealer inquiries are welcome.

I Met More Ghosts

at Gettysburg

A Journalist's Paranormal

Journey Continues

By Don Allison

Faded Banner Publications

Bryan, Ohio

Library of Congress Control Number: 2018957307

I Met More Ghosts at Gettysburg: A Journalist's Paranormal Journey Continues

Don Allison

Cover design by Stuart Rosebrock

ISBN   978-0-9659201-7-9

First Printing

I dedicate this book to my family, whose support of my writing endeavors has been invaluable, and in the memory of my Aunt Patricia (Allison) Zwayer, one of my most ardent fans whose encouragement and feedback is sorely missed.

Acknowledgments

I wish to thank all my family members and friends who encouraged me to write my first book exploring unexplained phenomenon, "I Met a Ghost at Gettysburg: A Journalist's Journey Into the Paranormal." Without their urging, I would never would have had the courage to share my rather incredible experiences and what I had learned about those encounters. Actually, without their help and support as I grappled to make sense of it all, I might still be questioning my own cognitive skills.

I am indebted to my parents, Jimmie and Charles Allison, for their wisdom and guidance. They taught me to be confident in myself, and showed me the incredible value of education, hard work and perseverance. My parents also encouraged me to enjoy and appreciate what life has to offer, and they have provided total support in all my endeavors. That they remain a part of my life is one of my greatest blessings.

My wife, Diane, has been a rock when it comes to my writing. She most of all encouraged me to share my paranormal encounters with the world, both in "I Met a Ghost at Gettysburg" and in this follow-up volume. As we both have encountered unexplained phenomenon again and again in our historic Ohio home, and at Gettysburg, Pennsylvania, we can reassure each other that our experiences indeed are real.

As always Diane has offered insightful critiques of my latest work, and has indulged my writing whims even at the expense of completing our home's restoration.

Our oldest son, Stuart Rosebrock, has once again lent his creative in support of my work, creating the cover for this volume. As I have said before, he seems to read my mind when it comes to the effect I desire with any given book design.

I also very much appreciate the input and hospitality of Mark Nesbitt. Both "I Met a Ghost at Gettysburg" and this project are better books because of his involvement.

Chet Crist of Flex & Flannigans in Gettysburg was instrumental in my decision to write "I Met a Ghost at Gettysburg" and has been very supportive of that work and this new volume. When I approached him at one point about reordering copies of some of my earlier books he declined, saying he was reducing his book inventory. "If you write a ghost book, I'll carry that," he said. When I said I was contemplating it, he told me to come back when it was finished. I did, and he was true to his word.

I also would like to thank Henry and Pat Foister and Kat Klockow of The Paranormal View radio show. They were extremely instrumental in introducing me to the world of paranormal researchers and enthusiasts. Others in the field whose guidance and assistance have been invaluable include Laine Crosby, Cat Gasch, Tiffaney Mason, Darcie McGrath, Mike Stevenson, Tinamarie Ronan, Robert Murphy, Skip Gibson, Jo Collier, Dr. Brian Parsons, Frank Lee and Pam and Steve Barry.

My good friend Mike Sutton, as always, has provided insightful feedback and contributions in my continued paranormal exploration. Mike's suggestions and input have been invaluable. Too, friends Bruce Zigler and

Shad Zulch have been understanding and supportive when I have had apparently paranormal experiences when they accompanied me during Gettysburg visits, and have graciously shared with me the fruits of their own research.

I owe a debt of gratitude to Jane Huffman, Denver Henderson, Pam Lash and others at the Williams County, Ohio, Public Library. They have gone out of their way to assist me anytime I have asked. I also am grateful for the assistance of Research Historian Timothy Smith and other staff members of the Adams County, Pennsylvania, Historical Society, as well as the staff of the Adams County Public Library for their assistance while I conducted research in Gettysburg.

To my coworkers at The Bryan Times in Bryan, Ohio, I would like to offer thanks for their feedback and encouragement regarding my book writing and publishing efforts. I would like to especially mention Diane Allison, Christopher Cullis, Don Koralewski, Ron Osburn, Dollie Conant, Heath Patten, Josh Ewers and Mike Sutton for editing this manuscript. Their professional assistance is a true asset to this work.

It would be simply impossible to list everyone who has supported me, provided input, shared their personal experiences or helped in any other way. To you all, I offer my sincere appreciation.

Finally, I'd like thank anyone who read "I Met a Ghost," and chooses to read this volume, with an open mind. There is much in this world that we do not understand, and we do ourselves a huge disservice if we fail to explore the unexplained and learn all that we can.

Table of Contents

List of Illustrations

Preface

Such a Thing as a Ghost?

It's a great enigma, really. Human cultures across time have expressed a belief in ghosts, yet there is no conclusive, generally accepted scientific proof that they exist. And what exactly is a ghost, anyway?

It seems if ghosts do exist, science would have found irrefutable evidence by now. Yet countless people throughout history – up to and including the present day – have experiences they cannot explain, and believe they have encountered what we commonly consider to be a ghost.

At some level most of us are afraid of our own mortality, and paranormal occurrences can be taken as a sign of encouragement, that perhaps death does not end our existence. We can see unexplained communication as evidence that our consciousness can indeed live on after our physical departure. Deep down we may want to believe, and this can alleviate at least some of that fear of taking our final breath.

On the other hand, some people are terrorized at the possibility of encountering a spirit. The thought of entering a supposedly haunted building can strike fear into their hearts.

To a degree I believe we all fear that which we do not understand. Be it dreams or premonitions that defy the odds of being a coincidence, sights or sounds that our logic says simply cannot be, when we contemplate those things almost all of us experience some level of fear. It can be so much easier, so much safer, do so much for our peace of mind, to simply turn our heads and ignore it, wait for it to go away and forget it ever happened.

I'll admit it. I experience fear over the paranormal. In fact, at one point not so very long ago I was nearly overwhelmed by fright.

In this case I was frightened not of spirits, but living people – more specifically of their reaction to the boxes of books in the back of my van. "What in the world have I done?" I asked myself as I slowly inhaled, then held my breath to calm my nerves.

I was driving out of the parking lot of Bookmasters in Ashland, Ohio, where I had just picked up the first printing of my book "I Met a Ghost at Gettysburg: A Journalist's Journey Into the Paranormal."

My wife, Diane, was in the passenger seat, but I didn't share my uncertainties with her. She has been my greatest supporter, and was among those who convinced me to write the book. Besides, what could I do? It was too late to back out now.

I am not easily frightened. Typically I keep a clear head about me, and only realize later that perhaps I should have been afraid. I believe that's what was happening here. I had come to the bold decision to write and publish "I Met a Ghost at Gettysburg," and now I was realizing that perhaps I should have been scared to death before making that move.

In my mind I could hear the howls of derision as I stood before crowds of potential readers, speaking to them about "I Met a Ghost at Gettysburg." I knew what was coming. "Ghosts?" they would say, laughing in my face. "You're out of your mind."

Maybe it's that fear of ridicule by their peers that leads some researchers to shy away from investigating the paranormal. Of course it can be far better to choose a safe area of research than to risk becoming a professional laughingstock.

For more than four decades I have carefully nurtured my reputation as a reliable, trustworthy journalist. Since the early 1970s, first with the former Stryker Advance weekly newspaper and later with The Bryan Times daily paper, I have built a career on winning the trust of my readers in Northwest Ohio. For more than 20 years I also have been a book author and publisher, my feet planted solidly on the ground as I wrote and edited books on Civil War and regional history.

While I drove home from Ashland in the fall of 2015 with those boxes of "I Met a Ghost at Gettysburg" stacked behind me, I envisioned that reputation entering a death spiral, picking up speed while plummeting toward the drain. To say I was very much regretting what I had done in publishing the book is an understatement.

After arriving home that deep sense of foreboding intensified as I unloaded the books and stacked them in my unfinished library. I had too much time and money invested in the books, and far too many resources committed to publicizing it, to back out now.

So I ignored my fears and forged ahead, already plotting how to recover from the professional catastrophe I was sure would come.

Now, looking back, I can very much appreciate the old saying that the true definition of courage is being afraid and acting any way. I don't see myself as particularly courageous, but by forging ahead in the face of almost overwhelming fear I achieved one of my greatest professional successes.

As it turned out my fears were totally unfounded. I can count on the fingers of one hand the people who have been openly hostile to me or "I Met a Ghost," and any jokes at my expense as I've addressed audiences have been rare indeed.

Instead audiences for my speeches have been open and friendly, receptive to my talks and the book's message. People have stopped me on the streets, in stores and at restaurants, and stopped by at The Bryan Times office to tell me in person how much they have enjoyed and appreciated "I Met a Ghost at Gettysburg." And the positive phone calls, emails, social media messages and even old fashioned letters have been incredibly gratifying.

Beyond that reception, I have learned that I am far from alone in experiencing paranormal encounters. Every time I have signed copies of "I Met a Ghost" or spoken before an audience, I have had people share their own unexplained experiences.

Sometimes people will tell their stories openly during my talks, often relating encounters similar to those I speak about. Not only are these stories informative to me, they are valuable in supporting my message to the audience.

Quite often, though, people are hesitant to share their personal experiences in front of others. More times than I can count I have observed people standing back, waiting patiently as others speak with me, ask questions and have books signed. Finally, once everyone else has left, they will approach me and privately share their own paranormal encounters.

Believe me, I understand their reluctance to relate their stories in front of others. That very fear held me captive for years before I took the plunge and began writing "I Met a Ghost at Gettysburg."

Now I feel I am providing very personal and valuable support to those who are perplexed over what they saw, or smelled, or heard or even felt, people who seem to be pleading "Please tell me I'm not crazy." I felt the very same way as I grappled with my initial paranormal experiences in my historic old home. Today I feel a deep connection with these perplexed individuals. When I can tell them they indeed are not losing their minds, that the experiences they had are in fact quite common, I feel like I am truly helping them come to grips with what happened to them, and in at least a small way making the world a better place.

After publishing "I Met a Ghost at Gettysburg" I didn't really expect to write another book on the paranormal. Instead I thought I was doing what I often do, explore a topic that has aroused my curiosity, write about what I learned and then move on to something new and different.

But this time, instead of finding the answers to most of my questions and feeling satisfied with my research, each potential answer to my paranormal queries seems to raise a dozen or more new questions.

In short, my experiences since publishing "I Met a Ghost at Gettysburg" have revealed an entirely new world to me, a reality that is truly awe inspiring. It's a quest I find I can't abandon, so it continues with this book.

My goal here is to encourage people to put aside their fears and open their minds to exploring a world beyond our day-to-day understanding. Ignoring or denying the unexplained doesn't make it go away. If anything, by doing so we cheat ourselves out of the chance to better appreciate the world around us, and to more fully explore what may well be laws of nature that we do not yet understand. Why not continue to tackle that age-old question, what happens to our personalities, our souls if you will, after we die?

Although I am not a scientist, it is my belief that scientific research may well illuminate these mysteries. Although it's true that our investigations thus far have not given us conclusive answers, I believe we should keep trying, keep coming up with new theories, new ideas and new research methods.

Should you have a background in science and my words can somehow convince or inspire you to focus your energies toward transforming the paranormal into the normal, I would be honored. Just think, you might well change the foundation of how we understand our world.

I have found my own journey down this path to be a fascinating one – wonderment and adventure replacing fear – and I very much hope you will come along as the ride continues.

Crew of the B-17 Mason and Dixon in May 1944. Kneeling from left are gunners Robert Humphrey, Walter Shipman, Robert Patterson and Everett Collier and radio operator Michael Sweeny. Standing from left are pilot Harvey Dickert, co-pilot Vernon Keilholtz, navigator Raymond Spahr, bombardier Jack Bryce and engineer Robert Levin. From the author's collection.

Chapter 1

Another Door Opens

"Can I tell you something?"

Until she asked me that question, I didn't even realize Tiffaney Mason had been standing a few feet away, taking in my conversation.

Actually, at that point I didn't even remember Tiffaney's name.

We were part of a scattered group near the Rose Woods at Gettysburg, and I had been immersed in a conversation with our group's guide, pestering him with questions about particulars of the fighting that had taken place there on July 2, 1863. I have been a student of the Civil War Battle of Gettysburg for most of my life, and I was intently focused on learning more about this specific point of the battlefield that I had previously visited only in passing.

My mind was very much back in 1863 at that point, envisioning the struggle there, and Tiffaney's question caught me totally off guard. "Sure," I finally replied, "what is it?"

She seemed a bit hesitant, as if unsure how to proceed. "You have someone with you," she finally replied.

"At first I thought he was a dead tourist, and I thought it would suck to be a dead tourist. But he said, 'No, I'm with him.' He was laughing, and saying 'Talk, talk, talk, useless information.'"

Tiffaney went on to describe my invisible visitor's appearance, saying he was wearing casual slacks and a beige windbreaker.

My mind went blank, and I didn't really know how to respond.

This exchange took place on a rainy Saturday afternoon, April 22, 2017. I was in Gettysburg that weekend at the invitation of the staff of The Paranormal View radio show.

The previous evening I had joined The Paranormal View group for dinner at the Fairfield Inn, a historic building on the route of General Robert E. Lee's retreat from Gettysburg in July 1863. I was one of more than a dozen people there, and had met only one or two others in person before that night. It turned out several in the group could be described as mediums or sensitives.

I must confess I am not terribly good with names, especially right after initial introductions as part of a group. My guess is that I probably appeared rather foolish to Tiffaney as I stood in the Rose Woods, trying to remember who she was, most likely staring at her with my mouth open trying to make sense of her comment that jolted me from out of the blue.

As I wrapped my mind around what Tiffaney had told me, my reaction was a very human one of trying to put the pieces of this puzzle into place. Casual slacks and a beige windbreaker is a pretty generic combination, especially when dealing with someone my age. Her overall description, though, did call to mind a close friend who had died slightly less than two years before. But this seemed so out of place to me – what connection could my deceased friend Jack, a lifelong Michigan and Ohio resident, have to me at Gettysburg?

As I looked back at the guide I had been peppering with questions about the Rose Woods, I realized he was wearing a Detroit Tigers baseball cap. Yes, Jack and I were diehard Tigers fans. We often watched Tigers games together on television, and we dissected the team's roster, performance and fortunes in great detail. Still, I shook my head at the stretch it would take for me to believe a Tigers cap brought my deceased friend to Gettysburg. It had to be simply a coincidence.

But I couldn't deny that Tiffaney had quoted this invisible companion as making lighthearted fun of me in a way that was very much the essence of Jack. He and I often shared insults – it was a friendly game with us – and I know Jack wasn't much interested in the Civil War. If Jack had somehow spotted a Tigers cap and was hoping to catch up with the team's fortunes, he would have found a Civil War discussion disappointing, and would have been inclined to give me grief about it.

Regardless, Jack at Gettysburg was just too far-fetched to give any more thought, I concluded. That is, until it dawned on me that Jack's World War II service as a bombardier aboard a B-17 aircraft had a definite Gettysburg connection. Three of his fellow crew members, I realized, were from the Gettysburg area. At the time of the war navigator Raymond Spahr and pilot Harvey

Dickert were Gettysburg residents and co-pilot Vernon Keilholtz resided in nearby Emmitsburg, Maryland. Ironically their aircraft bore the name Mason and Dixon, giving a nod to the Mason-Dixon Line that ran near Gettysburg, dividing North and South.

The crew Jack served with endured some harrowing times. They and their plane survived 35 bombing missions, a majority over Germany. They faced German fighter planes and anti-aircraft fire, and although the B-17 was sometimes damaged they always made their way back to their air base in England.

Jack and his co-pilot remained close friends following the war, and were the last two surviving members of the nine-man crew. Vernon died April 28, 2013, at age 90, two years before Jack passed at age 93 on May 12, 2015.

This, I thought, shaking my head, was simply beyond crazy. It was true that Tiffaney had not come up with Jack's name, but she had shared information with me that would have been seemingly impossible for her to know by conventional means, even if she had done countless internet searches and spent hours in the library.

The improbability of it all swept over me like a wave when I thought about a dream I experienced shortly before my Gettysburg visit. I dreamed I was on a local road trip with Jack, a very vivid, true to life dream. Jack's eyesight had been limited for years by macular degeneration, and he had been unable to drive. I would often pick Jack up to get together for coffee, share a meal or even check out a Toledo Mud Hens baseball game. After he was in the nursing home I would drive him to my house to watch a Detroit Tigers or Lions game.

In the dream I drove Jack around the nearby village of Edgerton, checking out various sites. That was appropriate, as Jack once owned the Edgerton Earth newspaper. Then we headed back to Bryan to have supper at the former Bryan News Stand, which had been our favorite hangout. Even though the News Stand has undergone ownership changes and remodeling in recent years, when Jack and I were there in my dream it was the old News Stand as it was when we spent time there.

Our food was being placed in front of us when I woke up. The dream was so real that it took a little while for me to get my bearings. I looked at my alarm clock, and realized it was nearly time to get up and get ready for work. Instead of rushing into the day I relaxed, closed my eyes and held on to the images of the dream.

To say I have very much missed my visits with Jack would be an understatement. I worked with Jack for years, and we had coffee breaks together nearly every afternoon at the News Stand. We shared stories of our journalism careers, talked sports and at times sought advice from each other. After Jack retired we often spoke by phone in between personal visits. We knew each other so well that I could telephone Jack, and when he answered I would skip any greeting and simply launch into a joke, and then hang up when I was done. He would do the same to me.

As I lay in bed contemplating the dream, it was if I had been granted one more visit with Jack. The warm feeling from that visit has stayed with me, even as I am writing this.

While I was composing "I Met a Ghost at Gettysburg" I very much missed Jack's counsel and advice. I'm missing it with this book as well.

For the rest of my stay in Gettysburg that spring, and quite frankly to this very day, Tiffaney's revelations have left me wondering how in the world – or beyond the world as we are aware of it – did she know what she knew? Why, nearly two years after his death, was Jack again becoming an influence on my life?

This was the opening of yet another new avenue of personal exploration. I realize this may all be one un- likely but possible series of pure coincidences, and my mind could be leading me astray while trying to make sense of it all. From a scientific point of view, I realize this proves nothing. I do believe it is worth contemplat- ing, however. And on a deeply personal level I certainly love the thought that perhaps I'm not without Jack's ad- vice and counsel after all.

Chapter 2

This Book Was Not to Be

Not so long ago there was no doubt in my mind. This book would never be written. Once I had published "I Met a Ghost at Gettysburg: A Journalist's Journey Into the Paranormal," I was done writing books on this particular subject.

Yes, I had encountered some very strange phenomena. Yes, I had explored it. Yes, I believed there is indeed something behind it, some scientific theories, and many intelligent, reasonable people conducting research. And yes, quite frankly, it had been an intriguing, interesting journey, and I certainly wasn't done learning more about it.

As far as my book writing was concerned, however, I had decided it was time to move on. I was still enjoying my newspaper work, and I loved writing my weekly On My Mind column in The Bryan Times. I also have some Civil War history projects still on the burner, and I couldn't wait to get to them.

Of course I had allotted time to promote "I Met a Ghost." After all I had invested months of time in researching and writing it, and a considerable sum in printing and prepublication publicity efforts. I reached out to arrange television, radio and podcast interviews, magazine and newspaper interviews, speeches and public appearances and even a book tour to Gettysburg.

Once the initial promotional rush was over, though, I expected to back off on the publicity. Sure, I would have to continue to push the book, but I also expected to move on to my historical writing endeavors. That, at least, was my plan.

I've heard the old saying, if you want to make God laugh, tell Him your plans. In this case, divine humor certainly seems to be in play.

Not only were people buying the book and telling me how much they enjoyed it, I found the feedback incredibly rewarding. Those attending my speaking engagements and book signings were looking to me to provide a sympathetic ear as they shared their own encounters. Those experiences have ranged from hauntings in their homes, to dream visitations by deceased friends or relatives, to disembodied footsteps and voices, to full-bodied apparitions such as phantom Civil War soldiers. I have been able to listen, and at times to help, to reassure, to provide some guidance. I felt more than validated in my own experiences as well. The more speeches I gave, the more people I reached, and the more the invitations kept rolling in.

Beyond that, I was attracting the serious attention of hard core skeptics, people who scoffed at the very idea of hauntings and ghosts. I was thrilled to see that my background as a journalist, coupled with my attempt to be as straightforward as possible and not reach any unproven conclusions, appeared to be opening some minds, even if just a crack. I felt like I was helping to advance the field of paranormal study in a meaningful way.

I received a real wake-up call as to the value of my work through an interview in November 2015 for the PBS station WBGU-TV in Bowling Green, Ohio. Steve Kendall, host of the show The Journal, invited me for an appearance on the hour-long show. My look at the paranormal was treated very professionally and seriously. One of the technical crew members of The Journal even shared his own paranormal encounter following the show's taping. On my drive home I felt elated. The show has aired many, many times since, and I have had countless people call, email or text me, and even stop me on the street or in the store, to tell me they saw the show and compliment me on the interview. Apparently that episode of The Journal has been shared with other public television stations, and people from as far away as Maryland and Massachusetts have told me they viewed the show as well.

I also have been interviewed for numerous radio shows and podcasts after "I Met a Ghost" was published, but one show in particular made a profound impact on me. In 2016 I was a guest on The Paranormal View podcast, with hosts Henry Foister, Barbara Duncan, Geoffrey Gould and at that time Kat Klockow. It was among my earliest interviews. I had an extremely good time during the show, and I felt like I had made a real connection with the hosts and audience. They asked insightful questions, were very open to my message, and offered some useful advice to me as a person relatively new to the field. I distinctly remember Kat Klockow telling me how she, too, wondered what she had done after her first book on the paranormal rolled off the press.

The Paranormal View is a weekly show, and at the end of the year they take two weeks off and run repeats of two earlier shows. At the end of 2016 they let me know that my interview was one of those two reruns. I felt honored, but I only later learned the true significance of that replay.

Kat Klockow, Don Allison and Henry Foister prior to a broadcast of The Paranormal View show from Gettysburg in April 2017. Courtesy of The Paranormal View.

A few weeks later The Paranormal View team invited me to an April investigation of the Fairfield Inn, a reportedly haunted location near Gettysburg. I was very intrigued by this opportunity, and I quickly said yes. This trip is how I encountered Tiffaney Mason in the Rose Woods.

It had been a ghost box conversation with some sort of intelligent energy claiming to be an Ohio captain from 1863 that – perhaps more than anything else – led me to write "I Met a Ghost at Gettysburg."

As it turned out, my experiences with The Paranormal View crew and associates during that April 2017 event served as yet another turning point in my writing life, as I truly did meet more ghosts – or experiences that we broadly interpret as ghosts – at Gettysburg.

Diane Allison taking K2 readings during an April 2018 investigation organized by The Paranormal View at the Gettysburg Brew Works. Author photo.

Chapter 3

I Am Part of a Long Line

As I was researching "I Met a Ghost at Gettysburg" I was intrigued by other writers who have taken a serious look at the paranormal. People with varied writing interests saw their careers take a new turn after they had experiences beyond the norm, or the encounters of others sparked their curiosity, and were so captivated they began exploring, researching and writing about these mysteries. Now I realize I am just one more in a long line of paranormal journalists.

Many are dedicated paranormal investigators – ghost hunters if you will – who focus first on investigating haunted locations and gathering evidence, and base their writings on their findings.

Regardless of what initially attracted them to the field, experiences with the paranormal, whether personal or shared with them by others, is a common denominator.

One of my favorite paranormal writers is the late Hans Holzer, author of at least 140 books on paranormal topics. His writings in the field are backed with experience as an investigative journalist and a doctorate in applied science from the London College of Applied Science. He taught parapsychology, and wrote, hosted and produced several television shows dealing with the paranormal, including NBC's "In Search of ..." According to one account Holzer was initially drawn to the paranormal by stories told to him by an uncle. He went on, though, to have a vast array of personal encounters. Holzer has investigated a wide range of places, including famous locations, historic sites, mansions, houses new and old and public places. His accounts of these investigations make for good reading, and I believe he was devoted to an attempt to follow the scientific method in sometimes uncharted waters. I find that Holzer's evidence and conclusions serve to collaborate many of my own experiences and beliefs.

I find a point that Holzer makes to be very telling: "Ever since the dawn of humankind, people have believed in ghosts." Writer after writer notes this same fact – belief in ghosts or an afterlife is part of every human culture that has left a written record.

Another author I find insightful is Loyd Auerbach. Although much of his background is in entertainment and television, based on his training, experience and expertise I consider him a leader in the field of parapsychology. He wrote a guide for investigators, "Ghost Hunting: How to Investigate the Paranormal," which I find very refreshing in its straightforward approach. In this book and subsequent writings he explains technology available to investigators and the fallibility of the human mind in interpreting experiences, and provides advice on how to differentiate between normal and the paranormal. He holds a master's degree in parapsychology, has taught in the field, and has been involved with the Rhine Research Center and the Parapsychological Association. Auerbach works to promote acceptance of parapsychology by the scientific community. He has said his interest in the paranormal dates to his childhood.

Brad Steiger is a writer recognized for his books on the paranormal. He, too, is a paranormal investigator, and through the years has made many radio and television appearances.

According to the "About the Author" information and introduction of his 2003 book "Real Ghosts, Restless Spirits, and Haunted Places," Steiger's interest in the paranormal was sparked by his encounters with unexplained phenomena in his home as a young child, and punctuated by experiences in the 1970s in a home where he lived with his wife and four children.

When veteran Pulitzer Prize-nominated print journalist Michael Clarkson wrote a non-fiction book addressing the paranormal, it surprised some people. He was drawn to researching and writing the book, "The Poltergeist Phenomenon: An In-Depth Investigation Into Floating Beds, Smashing Glass, and Other Unexplained Disturbances," after speaking with a man who had been at the center of a poltergeist case.

A number of us have one thing very much in common – we were writers, we had no interest in the paranormal, and then we had personal paranormal experiences.

Mark Nesbitt, perhaps best known for his "Ghosts of Gettysburg" series of books, is one example. Starting out, Mark's career interest was history – he was drawn to Gettysburg by his fascination with the battle, and in the 1970s he became a Gettysburg park ranger. "I was the bachelor at the time," Nesbitt told me in a 2009 interview, "so they moved me to the houses out in the park." In those houses – which saw the horrors of the July 1863 battle in which 51,000 American soldiers were killed, wounded, captured or listed as missing – the young ranger had experiences he couldn't explain. And he learned those experiences matched those of others. "Like babies crying in the house when there are no children," he said. "Doors that wouldn't stay closed, in one building."

Nesbitt left the park service in 1977 and began a freelance writing career. Initially his work focused on Gettysburg history, but eventually his pen turned to his paranormal encounters, and those others had shared with him. He remains involved in investigating the paranormal, and sharing his results and the experiences of others in his books.

As Nesbitt described it to me, park visitors and Gettysburg residents talk of hearing the sounds of battle on a still night, encounters with men in Civil War uniforms who disappear into thin air, the flash of musket fire on a distant hill, wounded men's cries for help on a dark battlefield hillside, encountering the odor of rotting flesh. They are not nutball cases, he said. "These are doctors and lawyers."

"Interestingly enough, they're tales I've heard before — the phantom battalion, the woman in white. There's a repertoire here of stories, and experiences, that are in common." And when the same things happen to different people in the same location or building, but years apart, he said, "that's what you call a haunting."

As Nesbitt sees it, "If you get enough apocryphal stories, it becomes data."

I especially feel a true kinship with Robert Dale Owen, who addressed the paranormal in his 1859 book "Footfalls on the Boundary of Another World."

Nothing I could find in accounts of Owen's early life foretold his interest in the paranormal, although he was more than willing to write about controversial topics. Born in 1801 in Scotland, he came with his social reformer father to the United States in 1825 and settled in the utopian community of New Harmony, Indiana. The younger Owen served as co-editor of the New Harmony Gazette community newspaper in the late 1820s. Later he penned a book promoting the generally unpopular concept of population control, and from 1831 to 1832 served as co-editor of the Free Inquirer, a New York City radical publication that tackled such controversial topics as abolition of slavery, redistribution of wealth, women's rights, universal suffrage, free public education and birth control.

Later Owen turned to politics, serving two terms in the U.S. House of Representatives from 1843-1847, sandwiched between stints in the Indiana legislature. He was considered instrumental in the founding of the Smithsonian Institution.

From 1853 to 1858 he was U.S. minister to the Kingdom of the Two Sicilies in Europe, appointed to that post by President James Buchanan. It was at that time, in Naples, that his attention was captured by occurrences he could not explain, including objects moving without apparent cause and an encounter with what he termed "an intelligent agent foreign to the spectators present."

Until he witnessed those unexplained happenings in the autumn of 1855, as he wrote in the preface to "Footfalls," he regarded the paranormal "as a delusion which no prejudice, indeed, would have prevented my examining with care, but in which, lacking such examination, I had no faith whatever."

In other words, he had to see it to believe it.

At that time spiritualism – the belief that souls of the dead can interact with the living – was very popular in both Europe and the United States, Even so, he had not delved into the matter before his personal experiences. He was so captivated by what he had seen that soon after he began immersing himself into the study of paranormal matters and felt compelled to share his research with the world.

Owen summarized his findings and conclusions in the "Footfalls" book: "For a time the observations I made were similar to those which during the last ten years so many thousands have instituted in our country and in Europe, and my reading was restricted to works for and against Animal Magnetism and for and against the modern Spiritual theory. But, as the field opened before me, I found it expedient to enlarge my sphere of research – to consult the best professional works on Physiology, especially in its connection with mental phenomena, on Psychology in general, on Sleep, on Hallucination, on Insanity ... on the subject of Human Electricity in connection with its influence on the nervous system and the muscular tissues."

Basically, Owen was attempting to undertake an approach based in the science of the period. "Gradually I became convinced that what by many have been re-garded as new and unexampled phenomenon are but modern phases of what has ever existed," he wrote.

Owen and I share a very similar approach. We both believe science holds the answers to paranormal mys-teries, and that the matter deserves further – and very serious – scientific study by professionals trained in the fields involved.

My own thoughts and my own situation today are re-ally not much different than what Owen faced in the 1850s – and although we have more technology and ev-idence stemming from those advances, I don't see that we are all that much closer to real answers – conclusive scientific proof if you will – than we were in his day.

In fact, what Owen penned in 1859 could just as easily be put forth today: "I aspire not to build up a theory. I doubt, as to this subject, whether any man yet living is prepared to do so (although many have, but they have not met scientific requirements for proof). My less am-bitious endeavor is to collect together solid, reliable building stones which may serve some future architect.

"Already beyond middle age, it is not likely that I shall continue here long enough to see the edifice erected. But others may. The race endures, though the individual pass to another stage of existence."

I must tip my hat to Owen, I couldn't have said it bet-ter myself.

Author Don Allison using dowsing rods near the Tros-tle Barn on the Gettysburg battlefield in August 2018. Don received "yes" answers to New York and New Jer-sey when asking where the respondents were from. The orbs visible here were clustered around Don only while receiving answers with the dowsing rods, not before or after. Courtesy of Leslie Policastro.

Chapter 4

Tennessee, Alabama, New York, New Jersey

Twice while in Gettysburg I was encouraged by para-normal investigators to try my hand at dowsing rods, and I was surprised by the results.

I was somewhat familiar with dowsing rods from previous experience in locating drainage lines. Basically, they are a set of L-shaped wires that can cross when the user encounters underground water or in answer to questions posed to an unseen energy or intelligence. My introduction to dowsing rods came in high school, when a teacher had our class use them to find a water line between the street and the school. All of us students ended up in a line, our rods crossed, and the experience made a lasting impression on me.

More recently I used dowsing rods to successfully locate my historic home's septic tank, and the gray water line leading from our kitchen. Interestingly, the rods also worked for my grandson, but not for my son.

My first encounter with dowsing rods in a paranormal investigation was on Saturday evening, April 22, 2017, with The Paranormal View group at the Fairfield Inn near Gettysburg. The previous evening while in the basement of the inn medium Cat Gasch had shared with us that she sensed the spirit of a Confederate cavalry-man from Tennessee who was wounded in the leg.

When I again found myself in the basement the following night, this time with a borrowed pair of dowsing rods, I asked a series of questions as a follow-up to Cat's experience. The first was "Is anyone here with us?" The rods crossed, signifying yes.

I had not really expected the rods to move, so I was surprised. I next asked, "Are you a soldier?" The rods again crossed.

Next I decided to mix up the questions, not exactly following what Cat sensed the night before. "Are you a Union soldier?" No movement of the rods. "Are you a Confederate?" The rods crossed.

"Where are you from? Virginia?" Nothing, and also no movement when I mentioned North and South Carolina, Georgia, Alabama, Kentucky, Mississippi, Arkansas and Texas. But when I said Tennessee, the rods crossed.

I tried the same approach again. "Are you in the artillery?" No movement. "Infantry?" No movement. "Staff officer?" No movement. "Cavalry?" The rods crossed.

"Were you hurt?" The rods crossed. "Where were you hit? In the head?" No movement. "In the shoulder?" No movement. "In the arm?" No movement. "In the stomach?" No movement." In the leg?" The rods crossed.

"Was your leg amputated?" At that point both rods pointed to my left, toward the basement wall, and the rods failed to move after any of my questions that followed.

Needless to say I was intrigued at this point, and a bit incredulous. I could not consciously replicate the same movement of the rods, try as I might. I could only get them to move if I obviously manipulated them. If I held them properly, loosely in each hand, I simply could not consciously force the same movement.

I must note it is possible, since I was thinking about the answers to these questions based on Cat's experience, that my subconscious mind created the rods' movement. But what exactly was at work here, I really don't know.

When I returned home I researched the order of battle for Lee's Army of Northern Virginia at Gettysburg, and found no Tennessee cavalry units listed. I found no Union Tennessee Cavalry units with the Army of the Potomac at Gettysburg, either. So I was left to wonder whether my mind or the mind of others there forced the rods' movement and there really was no soldier's spirit present, or whether the orders of battle were incomplete. Or, perhaps a cavalryman from Tennessee was there on detached duty or had joined a unit from another state.

When I was in Gettysburg on the evening of Friday, Aug. 10, 2018, I took part in an informal ghost hunt through contacts I made with the Facebook group Paranormal Gettysburg and Anything Gettysburg Related.

We traveled to Sachs Bridge, famous for reports of paranormal activity, and walked around the area and onto the bridge. A member of the Facebook group, Leslie Policastro, lent me a pair of dowsing rods.

I tried out Leslie's dowsing rods on the north side of Sachs Bridge, along the field hospital area east of the roadway. I first asked, "Is anyone here with us?" The rods crossed. Since I had family members from Alabama who fought at Gettysburg, my next question came easily to mind. "Anyone from Alabama?" The rods crossed. "Fifteenth Alabama?" The rods crossed. "Forty-seventh Alabama?" the rods crossed. "Forty-fourth Alabama?" The rods crossed. "Fourth Alabama?" The rods crossed. When I turned and faced toward the bridge and asked "Where are you?" the rods pointed to the left, into the field. When I asked the same question with my back to the field, the rods swung around to each side of me and pointed back at the field. I truly felt an energy at work beyond myself as the rods moved, whether that actually was the case or not.

The Alabama units I mentioned were from Evander Law's Alabama Brigade, so it made sense that some of their wounded would make their way to a field hospital near Sachs Bridge, which some in Lee's Army crossed to begin their retreat south after Gettysburg.

None of my queries regarding Union men or states were followed with movement of the rods.

Again this time, I was not expecting the rods to work, and their movements left me puzzled. Still, was my sub-conscious the source of the movement?

We then traveled to an area west of the Trostle farm on the scene of the second day's fighting. The brick Trostle barn is a familiar battlefield icon due to a hole on the west end caused by a cannonball. I took a number of photos in the area, a few of which had orbs, but nothing I considered as real evidence. Here I again tried the dowsing rods.

"Is anyone here with us?" The rods crossed. "Are you a soldier?" The rods again crossed. "Where are you from?" I next asked. But when I named off all the Confederate states I could think of off the top of my head – Alabama, Texas, North Carolina, South Carolina, Arkansas, Mississippi and Virginia – the rods did not move. I started naming Union states, and at first there was no movement of the rods. When I named New York and New Jersey the rods crossed, but not for any others.

"Where did you fight?" As I faced east toward the Trostle Barn, in the direction the Confederates attacked, the rod in my left hand pointed to the left, and the rod in my right hand swung to the right. At first I did not understand this. But I thought it over for a bit, then I wondered if perhaps I was near the line of battle as the Yankees retreated toward Cemetery Ridge. I continued my questioning. "New Jersey?" The rods crossed. "Where did you fight?" The rods both swung to the right. "New York?" The rods crossed. "Where did you fight?" The rods pointed to the left. At this point I was shaking my head, wondering how this could be.

While I was asking these questions Leslie was taking photographs, and later she showed me her shots. Like my own photos, most of hers showed few or no orbs. But in some of the images taken while I was getting movement of the dowsing rods, I am surrounded by orbs. I know many believe orbs do not signify anything paranormal, but the timing and sheer number of these orbs caused me to think long and hard. Perhaps my subconscious mind could be behind the rods' movement, but what about the uncanny appearance of a literal swarm of orbs at the same time, orbs that for the most part were not present in photos taken before and after?

Other spots we visited that evening resulted in little or no paranormal evidence, including Iverson's Pits and the Michael Trostle farm, a Union field hospital on Sachs Road where wounded troops in the Second, Third, Fifth and Sixth Corps were treated.

After I returned home I researched the area near the Trostle barn where I received the dowsing rod responses. The "Gettysburg Campaign Atlas" by Philip Laino indicated that, from my vantage point facing east toward the Trostle barn, there were indeed New York troops at that location and to my left, including the 39th, 150th, 125th and 126th New York infantry regiments. The atlas also showed that New Jersey troops indeed fought to my right – the closest was the 7th New Jersey Infantry.

Yet, a jumbled mass of retreating Union troops from several states passed through the area, and Barksdale's Mississippians were among Confederates fighting there. In that light, several Union state responses would have been appropriate. However, I must note that the New Jersey and New York responses were the two most accurate ones, based on Laino's atlas.

Can I look at this as evidence of spiritual activity, of the ghosts of long-dead Civil War soldiers, or is it due to chance? And what about the timing of the orbs? Is it simply a series of coincidences, against the odds but yet possible? Either way, my experiences that night certainly are food for thought.

Many consider dowsing or divining rods as a pseudo-science, whether searching for water, graves, underground material or spiritual energies. Researchers chalk up any results to sheer chance, or to muscle movements caused by subconscious mental activity. In effect, studies indicate people want the dowsing rods to work, so subconsciously they make them work. This is the same explanation scientists give for the movements of the planchette on a Ouiji board.

Some in the paranormal field, however, swear by dowsing rods, believing electromagnetic energy is the source of the movement. The UK Groundwater Forum gives a nod to this theory, at least when underground pipes are involved, concluding it is not possible to completely discard the idea: "Some people seem to be able to locate buried pipes with the aid of rods or twigs. One theory for this is that the muscles in the body react to some electromagnetic effect caused by the presence of the metal or the water flowing through the pipe; the rods then amplify this effect so that the searcher becomes aware of them."

A Popular Mechanics story supports this idea as well, noting "there is ample evidence that humans can detect small amounts of energy. All creatures with eyes can detect extremely small amounts of electromagnetic energy at visible light wavelengths."

This article notes that researchers analyzed the successes and failures of dowsers over a 10-year period in attempting to locate water in Africa, and concluded their success rate was impressive. "In hundreds of cases the dowsers were able to predict the depth of the water source and the yield of the well to within 10 percent or 20 percent," says Hans-Dieter Betz, a physicist at the University of Munich, who headed the research group. "We carefully considered the statistics of these correlations, and they far exceeded lucky guesses," he says.

Betz believes that electromagnetic energy resulting from water may be involved. Dowsers, he theorizes, may somehow sense this energy.

Despite scientists' contention that dowsing does not work, it is an ancient practice that will not die easily. There are even organizations worldwide, including the American Society of Dowsers, dedicated to dowsing. The society's website has links for dowsing in the news, and shares what it terms as dowsing success stories. The society even has its own quarterly newsletter, American Dowser.

The summer 1997 issue of American Dowser contains an article by Joe Farrell dealing with time spent by dowser Cecil Downing in the Triangular Field at Gettysburg. This field, near Devil's Den, was the scene of horrific fighting on July 2, 1863, the second day of the Gettysburg battle. The Triangular Field is the site of many reported electronic equipment failures, including cameras and video recorders, as well as claims of apparition sightings.

In an attempt to find a cause of these malfunctions and sightings, Farrell contacted geologist Robert C. Smith of the Pennsylvania Bureau of Topographic and Geologic Survey. Farrell questioned whether the geology of the field, more specifically the crystal structure of the diabase intrusion rock at the field, could result in naturally occurring magnetic emanations that could lead to the strange experiences there. "Bob said diabase didn't produce any such emanation," Farrell wrote.

According to Farrell, when Downing dowsed the Triangular Field he was not aware of the battle lines and troop movements through the area. Downing found and mapped areas he said were sites of emotional energy. Later, "Looking at the lay of the land in relation to the battle action," Farrell wrote, "he felt these were places where – in some, small groups, in others, individuals – men sought whatever shelter available or where they may have realized their final fate." Historian and "Ghosts of Gettysburg" series author Mark Nesbitt looked at Downing's findings and confirmed that these were areas in which Confederates from Texas and Arkansas engaged in vicious fighting with New Yorkers of the Union army.

OK, scientists conclude from overwhelming evidence that subconscious muscle movements do indeed cause the dowsing rods to move. But is it possible their research hasn't gone far enough to totally disprove dowsing's validity?

A common theory of ghosts and hauntings is that electromagnetic energy is involved. If dowsers can react to subtle amounts of electromagnetic energy given off by water, is it too far-fetched to at least consider the possibility that they react to other sources of this energy as well, as in the case of Downing's experience in the Triangular Field? Could the scientifically validated subconscious muscle movements causing the dowsing rods to move be a real response to an unexplained electromagnetic energy?

Perhaps and perhaps not, but I believe it is worth consideration and further research.

In making that assertion, I am backed by no less than Albert Einstein. He wrote in 1946 that "I know very well that many scientists consider dowsing as they do astrology, as a type of ancient superstition. According to my conviction this is, however, unjustified. The dowsing rod is a simple instrument which shows the reaction of the human nervous system to certain factors which are unknown to us at this time."

I know what happened to me. Using the dowsing rods I had credible answers to questions that I could not have knowingly answered at the time, and the idea leaves me very perplexed, and wanting desperately to know more.

Chapter 5

So Where's the Proof?

So what is behind it all, the dowsing rods and pendulums, poltergeists, phantom smells and sounds, objects moved without apparent cause, visible apparitions, out of body experiences and electronic voice phenonena? Is there one overall force at work, or a number of them? Or is it an interaction among various factors?

Wouldn't it be incredible to have the answers?

The theories seem about as plentiful and varied as the questions themselves. I have spent hour after hour studying books, articles and online postings, and I've concluded what I found could easily form a book all by itself – or even volumes of books. Some researchers propose that the energy of living people is behind much of the phenomena. Living individuals' thought waves, they say, are somehow picked up by others, or actually can cause objects to move. In some cases, such as poltergeists, I see this as a theory worthy of the study being devoted to it.

Some very learned people take that a step further, believing our personalities survive after our physical death, our souls if you will, and are able in some cases to interact with the living. As intriguing as this is, no one has been able to provide irrefutable scientific proof.

Others theorize that some sort of time warp is involved, that past and present can somehow overlap. As this theory goes, we may hear footsteps that indeed are very real, but originated 150 years ago. We may see a disembodied torso and head, which is the only part of the body passing through the veil of time. Perhaps we may even smell the perfume worn by a person who was present at the spot decades earlier, according to this theory.

I find this very intriguing on another level. Might the person making those footsteps in 1869 also be hearing the song "Free Bird" playing on the sound system in our living room now – a truly ghostly encounter both past and present? In other words, as incredible as it may seem, are the sounds or other manifestations we experience coming from the past, or could they be instead from the future?

Bizarre? Yes. Impossible? Perhaps not. After all, some of mankind's most incredible discoveries come from thinking outside of the box.

Metaphysics may well be a vehicle to providing some answers. But by its very definition metaphysics is a branch of philosophy, not science. As defined by oxforddictionaries.com, metaphysics is "The branch of philosophy that deals with the first principles of things, including abstract concepts such as being, knowing, identity, time and space." Although scientific concepts are involved, a metaphysical approach poses serious obstacles if the goal is immutable scientific evidence regarding the forces of nature involved.

Quantum physics, which on the other hand is a recognized science, also may reveal answers. At its basic level, quantum physics deals with the smallest scales of energy and subatomic particles. It is based on the concept of wave properties of the elemental particles.

I will be quite frank, much of what I have read about quantum physics stretches the abilities of my comprehension. But I believe it is good to be challenged. It is the only way we can ever find answers in the paranormal field – and as much as my mental capabilities are exercised by quantum physics, I am also intrigued.

Please bear with me here as I delve briefly into a very significant quantum physics finding, the oft-cited double slit experiment. This trial involves projecting a laser through two slits in a flat surface onto a screen behind. The slits interfere with the paths of the light waves, creating alternating light and dark bands on the screen.

To the untrained eye this may not seem significant. But that result puzzled scientists because the light did not behave as mechanical physics would predict.

Light is made up not just of waves, but of particles called photons. For the slits in the experiment to create the alternating light and dark bands, physicists concluded these tiny photons must somehow pass through both slits *at the same time.*

Even weirder, scientists have tried to observe a single photon. When detectors are placed in front of each slit to determine which slit the photon actually passes through, the light and dark bands don't show up at all. Regardless of what the scientists may do in trying to observe the photon, the interference pattern fails to emerge. In effect, physicists are demonstrating that the simple act of *observation* by humans affects the behavior of the photons.

And weirder still, in a variation of the experiment a researcher's simple effort to detect a photon can actually change the photon's behavior retroactively, in effect changing an event that already occurred.

Talk about a time warp ... wow!

In effect the double slit experiment holds several significant implications. For one, it appears the light particles can do what they want, as if they have a form of consciousness all their own. This is energy making up its own mind, even though no physical brain is present. Beyond that, the act of human observation affects that "decision" the photons reach as to their behavior. And as incredible as it seems, the experiment also shows that human thought can *retroactively* influence the photons' behavior.

As I said, it looks like quantum physics may hold a key to unlocking these great mysteries of our world.

One branch of science, parapsychology, is devoted to exploring answers to paranormal phenomena. According to the Rhine Research Center, "Parapsychology is the scientific study of interactions between living organisms and their external environment that seem to transcend the known physical laws of nature. Parapsychology is a component of the broader study of consciousness and the mind." Parapsychological research focuses on five distinct areas: **telepathy**, or mind-to-mind communication; **clairvoyance** or knowledge of objects, people or events that are hidden via space or time; **precogni-**

tion, or knowledge of an event that has not yet occurred; **psychokinesis**, the mind moving or interacting
with matter; and **survival studies** looking at human
consciousness and whether consciousness survives after death of the physical body.

The Rhine Research Institute describes parapsychology as "bridging the gap between science and spirituali-
ty." It covers the gamut of paranormal occurrences,
from mediums to reincarnation, out of body experiences
to apparitions, and mind over matter to ghost activities.

Mainstream science is often extremely skeptical of
parapsychology. According to Psychology Today, "Crit-
ics of parapsychology cite a lack of evidence of paranormal activity and difficulty repeating findings. Yet a
fascination with the unexplained persists." Some people
believe parapsychology has been treated unfairly by
those in other scientific fields, yet others maintain it has
been given more than a fair shake.

Without irrefutable scientific evidence as to cause and
effect of incidents considered paranormal – that is beyond normal – a solid understanding remains beyond
our reach. I know some people conclude that scientific
study of an afterlife, or even curiosity about hauntings,
flies in the face of their religion. I once dealt with the
comments of an antagonistic minister during a talk before a service club, and others in the paranormal field
have shared similar experiences. But conflicts between
science and religion have been going on for centuries,
and I don't believe that should stop our inquiry. In fact,
scientific discoveries once considered to be heresy have
long since been universally accepted by the faith com-

munity as laws of nature. Science and religion, I believe, need not be mutually exclusive.

I do not have the tiniest shred of doubt that some of the things that have happened to me are very real, even if we don't know the cause behind the phenomena. Seated right where I am sitting as I write this, I heard heavy footsteps coming down the hall behind me. Although I knew I was home alone, the steps seemed so real that I first believed my wife had returned home early. When I said hello, the footsteps stopped. I got up, walked to the door of my office and looked down the hall, and no one was there. As soon as I returned to my chair the steps resumed, and then entered my office.

As the steps passed to my right, within arm's length, I felt a very distinct chill in the air beside me. The steps at this point were between me and a lamp on my desk, and that light cast a semi-transparent moving shadow on the wall to my left, that resembled the shape of a human, including a head. Those clear footsteps continued past me and on into the adjoining parlor, stopping in the middle of the room.

I am not crazy, I did not lose control of my senses. I know something very definite happened, just as at other times when I have been touched when no one was present, heard disembodied voices and even conversations, and had electronic devices and lights turn off and on by themselves. I swear on my honor and reputation that these things very much did happen.

What I don't know is what was behind it all. I fervently hope, though, that eventually we find more answers.

Chapter 6

Skepticism Remains Important

Before, during and after writing "I Met a Ghost at Gettysburg," I have strived to find natural causes for my mysterious experiences. In some cases I discovered the wind, a bird trapped in a chimney and even braking tractor-trailer rigs on the nearby highway created initially mysterious noises. For the most part, though, I have been left in the dark as to the true causes.

As part of my ongoing quest to uncover anything I may be missing, after "I Met a Ghost" was published I reached out to Benjamin Radford, a noted advocate of strict application of the scientific method to paranormal research. I was eager to lay my encounters before an experienced, accomplished skeptic and see what he had to say.

Radford was kind enough to speak with me briefly by telephone. He raised what I considered excellent questions, especially regarding my experiences with a "spirit box" at Sachs Bridge in Gettysburg.

During that Sachs Bridge incident back in late March 2015, paranormal investigator Destynie Sanchez led my grandson Connor Rosebrock and I on what was to have been a two-hour ghost hunt. This is an investigation commonly provided to tourists for a price, but offered to me as part of a courtesy package provided by Gettysburg tourism officials because of my role as a journalist. Among the equipment Connor and I chose to use was a spirit or ghost box, in essence a device that quickly scans radio stations. The theory is that the white noise created by the ghost box creates a medium for comments and responses from intelligences with no apparent physical presence.

For the first two hours of that investigation I had been underwhelmed. We received one intriguing response from the ghost box – an accurate reply of "blue" in response to a question as to the color of jacket one of us was wearing, and claims by Destynie and Connor of observing moving shadows nearby. But before we were done we began receiving – and continued to receive – what sounded like many clear, intelligent answers to our questions.

I told Radford my immediate reaction was that the company sponsoring the investigation was hoaxing me, seeking to get a good review from a journalist. However, I told him I had not been able to figure out how they may have done so.

His response somewhat surprised me. He did not think it was a hoax. Rather, Radford questioned my perception of the spirit box session. He addressed the fallibility of the human mind. Were we perhaps hearing answers because we wanted to hear answers, he asked, and making out words through the static when none existed?

Our scheduled two-hour Sachs Bridge investigation had been within five minutes of being over when we started getting numerous spirit box replies, only after the last of the other ghost hunters left the bridge and we had the historic structure to ourselves. When Destynie asked "How many of you are with us?" we received what I considered a very clear "Seven ... eight ... nine" response.

To this, Radford said he considered it strange that the voice counted off, rather than giving a straight answer. That is an insightful observation, and I considered it carefully. In thinking it over, however, I can see the possibility of this happening in an informal, mingling group of people. Perhaps a person would have to take stock of the number if it is dark, people are coming or going, and there are others around the area. Still, Radford had a point, it was an unorthodox answer.

I relayed more details of the spirit box replies to Radford, noting that when my grandson asked, "Can you play for us?" we began to hear clear guitar music, eventually with a higher pitched string instrument and harmonica joining in.

 Radford's response to my description of the music had also occurred to me earlier when I researched how the ghost box works. He asked if perhaps we were hearing bits of music coming through as the ghost box scanned radio stations, and misinterpreting it. During that evening I had noticed this very effect – snippets of music no more than a note or two – coming through over the device. I told Radford the music I described to him was much different than the radio station blips – steady music over several measures, fading out and intensifying, fading and intensifying again for what seemed to me like minutes.

I shared with Radford that we received many clear answers and statements through the box before the evening was over, interspersed with some we could not make out. Radford continued to ask me very pointed, pertinent questions, and shared much food for thought. For one, he asked if we were "cherry picking" the best of the responses. I had to say, to a degree, yes. But I noted the majority of the responses we were receiving at one point were very clear.

Radford was in effect talking me through the process of closely examining my experience at Sachs Bridge, challenging my assumptions and pointing out the tendency of humans to take shortcuts in mentally processing events, trying make sense of them based on past experience. A good example of this is pareidolia, the tendency of people to see meaningful images in random visual patterns. This explains how we make out shapes and faces in clouds.

At the end of our brief conversation Radford was very gracious, noting that he couldn't say for sure what we experienced, because he wasn't there. I was thankful that he had offered an extremely valuable tutorial on evaluating evidence, and taking into account the fallibility of the human mind.

Some of the thinking points he raised were ones I had considered earlier, but not as deeply as I did as he questioned my assumptions point by point. He sets the bar high, insisting on use of the scientific method and ruling out normal causes for seemingly paranormal experiences, and that has great value. I remain very grateful to Radford for taking the time to talk with me, and sharing his thoughts and observations.

Radford recommended that I read his book "Scientific Paranormal Investigation: How to Solve Unexplained Mysteries," and I did so. In it he addressed many of the points he raised with me, and also described how he debunked many paranormal "mysteries," often with simple, basic research.

In "Scientific Paranormal Investigation" he notes time and again that many researchers fail to check on the sources of ghost stories or mysteries before passing them on, and that their methods of paranormal investigation often lack solid basis in the scientific method.

After speaking with Radford and reading his book, and exploring the writings of many others questioning the validity of our perceptions of paranormal events, I have thought long and hard about my Sachs Bridge encounter and my other experiences.

Don Allison on Sachs Bridge in 2017, near the spot where he, his grandson Connor and investigator Destynie Sanchez experienced ghost box conversations and music in 2015. Diane Allison photo.

Chapter 7

A Matter of Coincidence?

A part of me would love to discount the entire night on Sachs Bridge in the spring of 2015 as simply misperception. Concluding that we cherry picked evidence, wanted to receive responses on the spirit box to the point we heard words when nothing actually was there, and that we allowed our minds to misguide us, as Benjamin Radford suggested might have happened, would make life a lot easier for me. Then I could stop investing so much mental energy trying to solve this puzzle, and alleviate considerable irritation and cognitive dissonance.

I definitely am open to the possibility of my mind leading me astray, and it is entirely possible I may have false assumptions about at least some of the things that happened to us at Sachs Bridge. But I can't just write off the entire experience, not with the questions that still loom so large for me. Parts of that night stick out in my mind so clearly that I simply can't discredit them.

For one, I was not looking for any results during what I considered as a touristy "investigation." In fact, I was not particularly open to results at all. I was there simply to entertain my grandson. As things occurred I was very much trying to discount the things that happened, not in a mindset of open acceptance.

And if the spirit box voices were indeed somehow a hoax, why did these replies show up only at the very end of the scheduled two hour session? Wouldn't these folks want to get the night over with, so they could go home on time? I certainly would not expect anyone to drag the investigation out needlessly. What also seemed significant to me was that the responses came only after we had the bridge to ourselves, and stopped after more people arrived.

The energetic spirit box responses to my questions about humor and music – two things that Civil War soldiers cherished – were very significant in my mind, as was the steady Civil War period music that distinctly had at least three instruments involved. And Destynie's facial expression as she reacted to the music seemed to be one of true wonderment, not something faked. My years of experience in journalism have helped me recognize when someone's reaction or statements simply don't seem right, and nothing in Destynie's demeanor seemed out of place or inappropriate that night.

I also am impressed with the sheer coincidence of another result of the session. While trying to determine the state our apparent spirit was from, when I said "Ohio" we received a very clear "yes." When I noted that Connor and I were from Ohio, the lights on the K2 electromagnetic field meters held by each of us both shot up to the highest level and stayed there for several seconds. We had tried throughout the evening to get the meters to respond, and could get only the smallest blips even when we held our phones up to the units. To add another level of coincidence, the meter held by Destynie did not register anything at that point.

The last response we received from the spirit box came after Destynie asked, "Were you hurt?" I simply cannot adequately describe the deep scream of agony that came through the box. Just thinking about it still sends chills down my spine. The sound of a woman crying after that scream took away all my energy, and any desire to continue the session. The sounds were too distinct for me to attribute them to static or radio blips.

Perhaps the most difficult part of that night for me to reconcile is the name we received over the spirit box. When Destynie asked for a name we received a three-syllable answer, and the middle syllable was an "ahn" sound. She asked repeatedly for the name, even saying, "Can you enunciate more clearly?" and we kept distinctly hearing the three syllables but the "ahn" remained the only part we could fully understand.

As I explained in "I Met a Ghost at Gettysburg," I expected to put the matter to rest when I got home and began researching the historical record for Gettysburg. At first I looked into whether any Ohio captains in fact were killed or mortally wounded at Gettysburg. I learned there were seven. When I came across the name Mahlon Briggs – the three syllables, "ahn" in the middle – it all seemed to click solidly into place for me. No other names meeting the criteria came even close.

Mahlon Briggs was a 24-year-old captain in the 75th Ohio Volunteer Infantry Regiment when he was wounded on Barlow's Knoll on July 1, the opening day of the Gettysburg battle. He was captured by the Confederates, and died as a prisoner on July. 3. Is this proof of the voice's identity? Of course not. But is it intriguing – even compelling – food for thought? In my mind, yes. Briggs' name matching the spirit box emanation could be a coincidence, but it seems a very unlikely one.

If anyone can shed more light on these points, and can help me prove "normal" causes, please give me a call. I would love to hear from you.

I'm sure most of us have heard the infinite monkey theorem regarding coincidence, that a monkey typing at a typewriter long enough would eventually recreate the entire works of William Shakespeare.

Perhaps the chimp typing thr night I was at Sachs Bridge did not recreate an entire Shakespeare play, but it seems to me the creature certainly did go a long way toward composing a compelling scene.

Chapter 8

The Paranormal View Crew

"I Met a Ghost at Gettysburg" had been out for more than a year when I was invited by The Paranormal View radio hosts to take part in their spring 2017 investigation at the Fairfield Inn near Gettysburg. Simply visiting the inn, even more than the prospect of investigating its reported hauntings, was appealing to me.

The Fairfield Inn dates to 1757, and is one of America's oldest continually operating inns. Located in downtown Fairfield, the inn was right along the Confederate Army of Northern Virginia's retreat route, and Gen. Robert E. Lee is among officers who rode past the building following the Battle of Gettysburg. The inn, as did so many buildings in and near Gettysburg and along the rebel army's return march south, had served as a hospital for the wounded.

Actually the scene outside the Fairfield Inn as the Confederates passed was at times one of horror. A train of wagons miles long carried the Confederate wounded, many of whom groaned or screamed in agony as the wagons jolted along the rutted roadway in the rain that followed the conflict.

I arrived at the Fairfield Inn having never before taken part in a large group paranormal investigation. Beyond viewing examples on television and engaging in in-depth discussions with experienced investigators, my only experience was in joining Connor and Destynie at Sachs Bridge and a bit of impromptu investigating on my own or with my wife or friends. As a newbie I was both intrigued and a bit intimidated when I met The Paranormal View show personnel and their other guests for supper that Friday evening, April 21, 2017.

We went around the room introducing ourselves, and I found it interesting that several members of the group were described as sensitives or mediums. I had very limited contact with mediums up to that point, and I looked on this as a learning experience. I also found that the group was very friendly, and I soon was very much at ease and enjoying myself.

After eating we split into smaller groups for investigating the inn. My most memorable encounter during that evening's investigation was Cat Gasch sensing spirits in the basement, including a runaway slave and the Tennessee cavalryman I wrote about earlier.

Our second investigation Saturday night proved more active. Not only did my try with the dowsing rods in the basement seem to validate Cat's experience, we also received some very interesting readings on a K2 meter in one of the rooms.

Other investigators said they had contact with a spirit who liked to have fun with technology. As our investigation was winding down the small group I was with entered one of the rooms. At that point in the night we were getting tired, and I know I was about ready to quit. However, I am glad we waited.

Tinamarie Ronan, one of the mediums, said she sensed something in the corner of the room. She was holding a K2 meter, which senses electromagnetic energy, and one or two of the lights lit up when she approached the corner. She asked the entity to light up more of the lights. If you want to entertain us ghost hunters, she said, all you have to do is light up the lights.

About half the lights lit up. Tinamarie continued to encourage the entity, and she kept getting a response.

Up until then I had been much more of an observer than an active participant in the investigation, given my inexperience, but here I decided to jump right in. "You're just laughing your ass off right now, aren't you?" I said, adding to Tinamarie's encouragement. The lights flashed about three-fourths of the way up. "Come on, you're just laughing your ass off!" Tinamarie asked the entity to take the lights to red and it happened. The lights lit up all the way to the top, and kept flashing to the top as I started laughing and kept adding to the banter, "You're just laughing your ass off!" By now we all were laughing, and kept at it until the entity apparently tired of the game.

We all were tired by then, and soon we called it a night.

Later I contacted Tinamarie for her recollections from the Fairfield Inn investigation. She informed me she encountered several spirits that weekend, including a young soldier interested in the technology of her phone, a well-spoken African American gentleman and a well-dressed young African American woman.

Tinamarie recalled that we were on the third floor when we encountered the spirit with a sense of humor. "By now it was late and we were in our final room," she noted, "which was the room my brother Todd was stay-ing in that night ... Shortly after being in the bedroom I started to have my K2 light up. I checked that it was not reacting to anything electrical in the room, the floor be-low it or to wiring above the room.

"Every time my K2 lit up I and everyone else in the room got excited. So I said to the ghost, who felt male but was not appearing to me, if he wouldn't mind mak-ing the lights on the K2 come on again. Well he did. Again, we got all excited. We were interacting with a spirit!

"I was practically giddy not just because of the K2 lighting up but that I could show my brother that yes you really can get results from the equipment like I had said. I asked the spirit if he wouldn't mind lighting up the K2 again but to only the orange light in the middle. Sure enough the K2 only lit up to the orange color. I was clapping my hands and looked like a kid on Christmas morning! I asked the spirit if he could light the K-2 up all the way to the red this time. He did. And again squeals of excitement, exclamations of jobs well done and clapping from all of us.

"You could practically hear the spirit begin to laugh at us for our reactions for doing this simple task. I said thank you to the spirit and said 'I know you've done this for us several times but can you just light up the ma-chine just one more time to red.' Sure enough it went straight to red.

"I swear at that time while we were all squealing with excitement that I heard a huge ghostly laugh at what he must of thought were a bunch of simpletons to get excited over a bunch of colored lights. We thanked him repeatedly and we got a weak, flickering display of orange light on the K2 and we realized we had probably tired the poor man out. He did not respond to any more requests after that. I realized that we had all seen and experienced with our own eyes that spirits can communicate with you and we definitely made one laugh."

That Saturday afternoon The Paranormal View had arranged a tour of the Gettysburg battlefield with an experienced guide. It was during this tour, while at the Rose Woods, that medium Tiffaney Mason told I me I was accompanied by a spirit that so much seemed to point to my friend Jack.

While the group was eating lunch at Tommy's Pizza I asked more pointed questions of Tiffaney regarding the Rose Woods spirit, and I was struck with her pleasant, low-key demeanor. She didn't seem at all like she was trying to impress me, or give me the "right" answers. She freely said "I don't know" to many of my questions, and was very open in discussing the incident.

This new experience with mediums was intriguing, so I asked Tiffaney and one of the then-hosts of The Paranormal View, Kat Klockow, if they could take me to any spots on Little Round Top where I may have had family connections. They didn't promise anything, but said they would try.

Kat accompanied me in my van, and when we parked and got out of the vehicle I let her lead. At that time I knew where some of my family members had fought with Alabama units, and she headed in the right direction. She walked slowly, as if taking in the atmosphere, and then confidently stopped at one of the spots. "Your family was here," she told me.

I'm not sure how she did it – she could have gone many different directions, but she took me to a spot on the battle line where one of my great-great-great uncles, Sgt. George W.C. Jarvis, fought with Company F of the 47th Alabama Infantry regiment on July 2, 1863. She said she sensed something there, and said she was getting the name William. I don't know what the W in my uncle's name stands for – I have seen a reference to a William that could have been him, but I am not certain. Kat also said she sensed gray among the rocks at the base of the hill, which ironically is where the 47th soldiers took shelter at one point during the fight.

Given the vast expanse of Little Round Top, the fact that Kat indeed identified a spot where one of my relative fought was significant to me. Granted, it could have been coincidence, especially considering I had more than one relative in more than one spot on Little Round Top, and I am not certain about the name. But the odds were definitely against her going directly to a correct spot.

So if factors other than coincidence come into play how did she accomplish this? I suppose it could be that I was giving off subtle, unconscious clues that she in turn could sense and act upon. Telepathy also could be a factor, that she was in effect reading my mind in determining a location. And given our limited knowledge at this point, it is not beyond the realm of possibility that the energy of my ancestor left an impression on the site or in the atmosphere, and Kat was able to tap into that.

On our way to Little Round Top Kat had received a message from Tiffaney noting that she was unable to find Little Round Top. She and her husband, Joseph, were unfamiliar with Gettysburg and they had driven to the wrong end of the battlefield. They were then near the Peace Memorial, and Kat gave them directions to Little Round Top.

Kat and I were still standing on the pathway on Little Round Top near the 47th Alabama battle line when Tiffaney and Joseph drove up to the base of the hill. Tiffaney got out of the vehicle and rushed up the path and past us. When she stopped she quickly kneeled in a shooting position, saying "This is it!"

Tiffaney was at the crest of the hill, within the battle line of the 20th Maine Infantry Regiment. She was in the middle of the area where the desperate, vicious struggle took place between the Maine men and the 15th Alabama Infantry Regiment for control of the left flank of the Union army on July 2, 1863. It is one of the most famous small-unit clashes of the entire Civil War, and as fate would have it members of my family were there.

My Great-Great-Grandfather, Frank Champion, fought there with Company I of the 15th Alabama. At least one great-great-great uncle, Robert (R.G.) Goodwin of Company K, also was there with the regiment.

Tiffaney told us she was sensing waves of blue and gray shifting around her, gesturing toward where the gray enveloped parts of the line, sweeping in behind the 20th Maine. I'm not sure how much she knew about the Little Round Top struggle – it is a well-documented fight – but she was very accurate as to the Alabamians shifting to our left and eventually coming in behind the Union line. When I confirmed the rebels had gotten behind the 20th Maine at one point Tiffaney quickly said "No!" She said someone named Joshua was coming through, telling her the Confederates did not get that far. She said she was seeing Joshua on a horse – not necessarily that he was on a horse during the battle, but signifying he was in a position of leadership.

Years after the battle, in which the 20th Maine held on to the hill by the skin of their teeth, the leaders of the respective regiments disputed each other's accounts of their units' accomplishments. William Oates, commander of the 15th Alabama, wanted to place a monument behind the Union regiment's position to indicate the Confederates' furthest advance. Joshua Chamberlain, the 20th Maine commander, denied Oates' claim, saying the Alabamians did not make it that far. Although postwar writings by both Maine and Alabama soldiers backed up Oates' claim, Chamberlain and his political connections won out. The monument proposed by Oates was never placed.

The postwar dispute between Oates and Chamberlain is documented, but I don't know how well it is known by most people, even those interested in the Civil War and Gettysburg. At the time I was on Little Round Top with Tiffaney I myself had only recently run across the commanders' exchange of letters, even though I had read much about the 20th Maine-15th Alabama fight, beginning as a child.

There again, I don't know what to think about this incident. Coincidence could have come into play, although again, given the vastness of the area that seems to me

unlikely. As far as subtle cues coming from me are concerned, Tiffaney didn't really seem to observe me, beyond my location. She may well have concluded to come
up the hill after seeing Kat and I standing there, but she
didn't even look at us as she rushed by and confidently
knelt further up the hill.

So was telepathy involved, or did she sense energy
left over from the long-ago violence? I thought that perhaps I had talked about my family connection there, but
I don't recall having done so. It was my first time with
The Paranormal View group and I was in a definite
mode of observing, listening and learning, not talking.
Once I decided to ask the mediums to locate a spot for
me, I made sure to avoid any such mention.

Since that day the questions have continued to perco-
late in my mind.

This August 2016 view depicts the terrain faced by the 15th Alabama as they attacked the 20th Maine up the slope of Little Round Top. Author photo.

Chapter 9

So How Do They Do It?

Before my April 2017 trip to Gettysburg my concept of sensitives and psychics had been based on reading, including accounts by Hans Holzer, and watching an occasional TV show. Since then I've thought a lot about such abilities, and my main question is a simple one: How do they do what they do?

Being a journalist, I didn't have to think very hard about my next step. I would just ask.

On Aug. 22, 2018, I spoke by phone with Tiffaney Mason about our shared experiences at Gettysburg. Tiffaney laughed when I reminded her of encountering my spirit companion in the Rose Woods. "I thought he was a dead tourist, because of his modern dress," she recalled, continuing to chuckle.

I asked if she actually saw the spirit with me that day, or just had a sense of him. In this case, she said, she saw him. "I physically see them, and I hear them," she said.

"I can take no credit. I am really just the messenger when they come through," she said, describing herself as "just a phone booth" for the communication.

Tiffaney said she also saw and heard the spirit she called Joshua on Little Round Top – the officer matching the description of 20th Maine commander Joshua

Chamberlain. "He said 'No, they did not break my line,'" she said. "I got the name Joshua, I saw him on the horse," she said.

When I asked her about the man's demeanor, she replied that "He seemed very friendly, but very direct."

Although Tiffaney said she really doesn't know anything about the Little Round Top fight, she has long been interested in the Civil War. "My heart has been with the South, ever since I was little," she explained. She told me she has ancestors from the South, including Louisiana and Alabama.

Tiffaney said she once saw a Civil War reproduction dress displayed in a shop, and was immediately drawn to it. She said she wanted to try it on, and the shopkeeper seemed surprised that it fit, even the outfit's jacket. "I felt at home," she said. "I was meant to be wearing this."

When I asked how she would describe her abilities, Tiffaney replied that "I am a psychic medium." She explained that she often sees and hears the spirits, but how they appear to her can vary. "It can be anything. It's dependent upon how comfortable the spirit is with me, and how much information they want to share with me."

"I was just a child," she replied when I asked when she first could see and hear spirits. "I was maybe in first or second grade. My mom is just very understanding – she said, 'They're just dead, they won't hurt you. Go back to bed.'"

So I asked, could someone like me develop those same abilities? "I think anyone can do what I do – it's not selective," Tiffaney replied.

Since the night at the Fairfield Inn I have had the opportunity to take part in another investigation with Cat Gasch, and to discuss various aspects of the paranormal with her. In addition, I have read her 2015 book "My Life Amidst the Paranormal," which offers insight into the life of someone who can see and hear spirits.

I spoke with Cat by telephone on Sept. 6, 2018, about her Fairfield Inn encounter with the Tennessee cavalryman.

Unlike Tiffaney Mason, Cat said she typically doesn't physically see or hear spirits. "I can honestly say that the number of actual visual manifestations of spirits I've seen, I can count on the fingers of one hand," she said. Rather, she explained, she experiences the contact in her mind's eye.

The cavalryman, a Pennsylvania soldier and a runaway slave were among the spirits Cat said she encountered in the Fairfield Inn basement. "They were definitely in distress," she said. "They were very rag-tag."

"As soon as I went down there I could see him ... in my mind's eye," Cat said of the cavalryman. "I can still see him." She said his clothing was not Confederate gray, but was more of the color a farmer would wear. She also said she sensed that he was wounded in the leg. "The way I can describe it, there was no bulk to his pant leg ... His left leg, all I could see was his left pant leg flapping in the breeze.

"His jacket was too small for him, and he had to button it at the top, the top one or two buttons, the rest of it was open, with his belly hanging out."

Based on my longtime study of Civil War uniforms I quickly realized that Cat, who had said she is not familiar with military dress of the period, had in fact accurately described an 1860s cavalry shell jacket. Shell jackets are very short by modern standards. And during hot weather – Gettyburg took place during humid days in early July – soldiers would button only the top button, and leave the rest of the buttons undone to help cool themselves.

When I shared that information with Cat she was surprised – she said she had no idea, and found it validating what she saw.

"He was telling me – when he was talking about where he was from, he actually was a little bit on the rude side because of my accent, or where I was from," Cat continued. "He knew I was from the North."

"He wouldn't even call me m'am," Cat explained. "All he did when I asked him questions was yes'm."

And, Cat said, "When I asked him 'Were you hurt?' he said yes'm. When I asked him where, he said 'In the leg.' He had very short answers for me. He wasn't trying to be rude, he was just letting me know, 'I really don't want to talk to you.'"

Until this conversation I had not shared with Cat that I returned to the Fairfield Inn basement the following evening, and using dowsing rods received the same information regarding the cavalryman.

Cat again found my comments as validating her experience. "That is probably one of the best things that can ever happen to us," she said, "when another person goes to the same location at a different time, and gets the same results.

"When something like that happens, it's great."

I also found it intriguing that wounded men were taken to the Fairfield Inn following fighting between cavalry forces near Fairfield. The 14th Virginia Cavalry and First Troop City of Philadelphia Cavalry skirmished on June 21, then a more involved clash July 3 involved the 6th U.S. Cavalry and the 6th and 7th Virginia Cavalry. Casualties July 3 included 28 wounded Federals and 21 wounded Southerners. There again no Tennessee units were listed, but that would not necessarily preclude a Tennessee man serving in a unit from across state lines.

As we were talking I told Cat about my then-recent visit to Gettysburg, and about walking back to the Slyder House near the Round Tops for the first time. She said she once went with two other paranormal investigators to the Slyder House, and after crossing the small foot bridge approaching the site she began feeling very ill. She understood her reaction, she said, when she was told it had been a field hospital at the time of the battle.

When I explained to her the house had been the field hospital for the Alabama Brigade, in which my own ancestors fought, Cat said she believes that explains her intense experience. At the time, she said, she did not know the site had housed wounded Alabamians, and the connection those men have to me. "Since I have been involved with paranormal groups, I've discovered there is one hell of a connection between all of us," she told me.

Cat said she has been aware of spirits since she was a young child. "When I first started seeing things, I was about five or six, but at that age you don't even think of telling anybody because you don't even know what it is."

She explained she was about 8 or 10 when she started seeing things that she realized other people paid no attention to, and obviously didn't see or hear. But at that time people who saw ghosts were considered insane, she said, and that frightened her. "I wasn't going to tell anybody because I didn't want to be put away."

"When I saw my first full-bodied apparition, I started looking into this," she continued. Even though still a child she took an adult point of view. She said she went to the library and asked the librarian for books about ghosts. Cat explained that she turned down children's books, and insisted on adult volumes.

Cat said she didn't mention anything about her abilities to anyone until she was about 14 or 15, when she confided in her older sister. "She, too, admitted she had been seeing and hearing things," Cat said.

I asked Cat if the ability to communicate with spirits is a selective ability, something you must be born with, or if people like me can develop it.

"I think you can develop it," she replied. "I think anybody and everybody has the ability – it's just a matter of believing that you can."

As an inquisitive journalist I am grateful to Tiffaney, Tinamarie and Cat for being willing to discuss their psychic abilities, and trusting me with their stories.

With my skeptical nature, my first impulse is to question what they are telling me, and to try to disprove their statements. In sharing these stories I did not cherry pick the best of them. I approached each one in a logical fashion. I asked detailed questions about the experiences I saw firsthand, looked into the historical record, and shared what I found.

I realize that skeptics can dissect these experiences, can say the statements from the psychics are not precise enough to prove anything, that any validations are pure coincidence, and that anyone taking anything significant away from these experiences is being misled by his or her own mind.

From a strictly scientific standpoint I realize I have not presented conclusive evidence of anything. But I have concluded that we are onto something here, and we need to pay attention and continue our quest for knowledge.

Slyder House, field hospital for the Alabama Brigade.
Author photo.

Chapter 10

So What's With These Alabamians?

When I first started down my Alabama road of dis-covery at Gettysburg I really had no clue as to just where it would lead, or how far it would take me. Actu-ally, I didn't initially realize it was a road at all.

I suppose the very beginning of this story was my honeymoon in November 1984. Making Gettysburg our first destination as a married couple actually was the idea of my wife-to-be. She knew how much I had want-ed to experience the town and the battlefield, so when she suggested it for our honeymoon I was quick to agree. Despite the fascination Gettysburg has long held for me, I had never been there.

We experienced nothing at all strange during our honeymoon. In fact there had been nothing at all in our lives that we considered paranormal until we pur-chased our historic 1835 home in Ohio.

As we worked to restore the house the paranormal activity we encountered both astounded and confused us. With our 25th anniversary approaching we looked forward to a break from our renovation work, and what better way to celebrate than a return trip to Gettysburg?

We decided to see if Mark Nesbitt would meet with us during our visit. Our goal was twofold – I wanted to in-terview Mark for a feature story for The Bryan Times regarding his "Ghosts of Gettysburg" books and para-normal investigating, and we also wanted to talk with him about the strange activity we were encountering at our house.

Mark agreed to meet us at his Ghosts of Gettysburg Candlelight Walking Tours headquarters on Baltimore Street in Gettysburg. He shared his own paranormal experiences in that building, and talked with us about our haunted house. At the end of this discussion Mark posed for a photo with Diane, but when I pressed the shutter the camera turned off. I turned it back on, and it turned off again. I was rather embarrassed having my camera malfunction in front of Mark, and even though I had placed freshly charged batteries in the camera just before the interview I replaced them again, to no avail. "It happens here all the time," Mark said, laughing. After perhaps a couple dozen tries I was able to capture two photos.

For the next few days we toured various parts of the town and battlefield, and my camera worked flawlessly – until the third day. Rain was falling and we opted to visit the Boyds Bears Store then located just off Emmitsburg Road south of Gettysburg. The rain continued to fall when we left Boyd's and headed back toward the park. However, as we spotted the boundary to the park the rain stopped.

Diane agreed with my suggestion to visit Little Round Top. Just as I flipped on the signal to turn right onto Confederate Avenue, the Lynyrd Skynyrd song "Sweet Home Alabama" came on the radio. I didn't think much about the song at first, but it certainly struck me as an odd coincidence when I saw the Alabama Monument on our right. Even though I had taken photos of the monument 25 years ago, I thought the fall foliage would make for a colorful background. So, with "Sweet Home Alabama" still playing I grabbed my camera, climbed out of the van and focused on the monument.

And my camera turned off when I pressed the shutter. Even though the "Sweet Home Alabama" strains now seemed a bit surreal, I concluded that any Gettysburg ghosts could be damned. My camera was definitely defective. But in a repeat of the Baltimore Street building scenario, I would turn on the camera, and it would turn off again as soon as I pressed the shutter. Not willing to be undone by a faulty camera, I kept continuing the cycle, and perhaps one time in a dozen I could capture an image.

We next made our way to nearby Little Round Top. Leaving Diane behind I made the quick climb from the road to the 20th Maine site and focused my camera for a photo of the unit's monument. Again the camera turned off every time I pushed the shutter. Once again I was stubborn, and with my persistence I could get the camera to work in about one out of a dozen tries.

I next turned my attention to the hillside, looking down at the approach taken by the attacking Alabamians. Now my camera worked fine – I took several shots looking down the hill, with no malfunctions. Curious, I turned back toward the Maine Monument, and again each time I hit the shutter the camera turned off. Looking back down the hill, the camera worked fine.

At this point I was shaking my head in disbelief. I got back in the car, explained to Diane my incredible experience with the camera, and we then continued our tour. The camera kept up its balky performance each time I tried to photograph a Union monument, and would work fine on other views, until after we were into the Wheat Field. That camera never repeated this performance again. I owned it for perhaps two years after that trip and never had a problem with it. I gave it to my son when I purchased a new one, and as far as I know he never had a problem with it, either.

Fast forward to April 1, 2015, and my visit to Gettysburg with grandson Connor. After our ghost box conversation at Sachs Bridge I thought back to Diane and my encounter earlier, and that evening we decided to make a quick visit to the Alabama Monument.

Motivated by my 2009 experience with Diane I had by this time looked into my family's Alabama roots, and learned that a number of men by the name of Jarvis and Champion – two of the family names on my mom's side – fought in the 47th, 48th, 4th, 44th and 15th regiments of Evander Law's Alabama Brigade. It was this Alabama brigade that formed up at the site now marked by the Alabama memorial, before moving to attack Little Round Top. Companies in these regiments were recruited from the counties where my Jarvis and Champion families resided, so I knew it was quite likely some of these men were related to me. I did not then know if any of them were with the brigade at Gettysburg.

After I parked in front of the memorial Connor and I both took photos of the monument. Then I turned on "Sweet Home Alabama" in the van's CD player. I began asking if anyone by the names of Jarvis or Champion were present, and as I read off individual names Connor took photographs of the monument, one shot after another as quickly as he could press the shutter. Then I turned off the music, and we both took more photos

All told Connor took 15 photographs of the monument while I called out the names. In the eighth photo, three unexplained spots of light appeared. The ninth photo shows two unexplained spots of light, and an indistinct orb. The final photo displayed one unexplained light and an orb. No photos taken before or after I played the music and called out the names contained anomalies.

With time in the park running short before the 10 p.m. closing time we got back in the van and made the short drive to the road between the Round Tops. We stopped at the base of Little Round Top, in the area through which the 15th Alabama charged to attack the 20th Maine on the slope of Little Round Top. We rolled down the van windows and I turned off the lights. Connor then quickly snapped five photos looking up Little Round Top. Nothing was visible to the naked eye, but the images Connor captured took us both by surprise.

The first photo shows several orbs visible on Little Round Top, some showing tails indicating a travel trajectory toward a pair of trees just up the slope from the van. In the lower left corner of the second image is a sort of yellow-orange-red mist at the base of these trees. In each of the next three photos this mist grows toward the center of the photo, and develops yellowish streaks of light. Viewing it on the camera screen, we saw what appeared to be a face in the mist in the final photo.

Meanwhile, my camera simply would not work. When I pressed the shutter nothing happened. The camera did not turn off, it simply would not snap a photo.

After Connor saw the orbs and mist in his photos, he began rolling up the window. "Grandpa, let's get out of here," he said. I told him my camera was not working and I wanted to take at least one photo, but he was insistent. "Let's go – now!" he said.

Finally, after several tries, my camera snapped one shot, and it had a bright red dot in the center of the photo. "OK," I told Connor. "I'm set, let's go." Connor and I share a sharp sense of humor, and we frequently needle each other for fun. At this point I couldn't resist a bit of levity, and I told Connor, "You know, rolling up a window isn't going to stop a ghost."

He caught the humor, and quickly shot back, "Maybe, but it made me feel better."

When we got back to the hotel we reviewed our photos. When we zoomed in we realized what appeared to be a face in one of Connor's shots was not, and the red dot in my last photograph was a reflection of the flash off a distant "wrong way" sign. Even then I realized orbs are dubious evidence when it comes to the paranormal, but the timing of the ones Connor captured was curious.

During a daylight visit the following morning we could find nothing to account for the colorful anomalies that appeared in Connor's shots, leaving us puzzled as to the source. What, we wondered, could cause both the cluster of orbs *and* the bright mist?

Chapter 11

Further Down the Alabama Road

Needless to say, Connor's photographs at the Alabama Monument and on Little Round top remained on my mind following our Gettysburg trip. Motivated once again by odd occurrences where the Alabamians formed up and fought, I began an in-depth search to determine if and how any of these men were related to me.

For about a month I devoted nearly all my spare time to online research on ancestor.com, including census and military records, as well as online searches of Alabama and military archives and obituaries, plus books on the Alabama Brigade.

I determined that three of my great-great-great-uncles, Benjamin F., George W.C. and James O.M. Jarvis, served in the 47th Alabama regiment, which attacked Little Round Top. In fact, they fought on the left flank of the 15th Alabama, and were part of that epic struggle against the 20th Maine and also faced the 83rd Pennsylvania Infantry Regiment to the 20th Maine's right. These men are brothers of my great-great-grandfather Newton Jarvis, who served in the 20th Alabama Infantry in the war's western theater. It is possible all three were present on Little Round Top. Records indicate they survived without major injury.

Men by the name of Jarvis or Champion served in the 48th and 44th Alabama that attacked Devil's Den and the 4th Alabama that fought at Little Round Top, but I still have not uncovered any evidence of relationship to me.

I was excited to discover that Frank D. and J.A. Champion were members of the 15th Alabama. Records show that John A. Champion was mortally wounded at Fredericksburg in 1862. But Frank Champion, it turns out, is my great-great-grandfather. He enlisted in Company I of the 15th Alabama in July 1861, and was paroled at Appomattox.

While reading "Stand Firm Ye Boys from Maine: The 20th Maine and the Gettysburg Campaign" by Thomas A. Desjardin, Shad Zulch came across a listing of Frank Champion at Little Round Top, noting that he was captured there, subsequently escaped and made his way back to his regiment. Ironically, Shad purchased the book while with me in Gettysburg in 2017. My subsequent research indeed bore that out – Frank was in fact captured at Gettysburg. He was taken to a prison camp at Point Lookout, Maryland, where he escaped on May 20, 1864, and made his way back to his regiment.

So there it is – proof that my direct great-great-grandfather indeed fought at Gettysburg!

I don't often use exclamation points in my writing. The fact that I used one to conclude the previous paragraph – the only exclamation point I use in this entire book – underscores just how amazed I am by this discovery.

And that's not all. Also serving with the 15th Alabama was my great-great-great-uncle Robert Goodwin, who also appears as Godwin, a private in Company K. His service records indicate he was absent from the regiment with illness from December 13, 1862, through July 3, 1863. He was, however, listed as captured in Pennsylvania on July 9, 1863, and exchanged on Nov. 1, 1863.

With the first discoveries of my family members' service a distinct connection with all the strange encounters on and near Little Round Top immediately came into clear focus. I simply cannot rule out that something beyond our normal conception is going on here.

Broken down individually, I realize every step of this sequence can be attributed to coincidence. For example, it has been suggested to me by skeptic Benjamin Radford that my camera was faulty when Diane and I were in Gettysburg in 2009. I agree it can't be proven otherwise, although the odds do seem stacked firmly against the camera functioning fine during years of heavy use before and after Diane and I took our anniversary trip, malfunctioning only at Gettysburg and especially Little Round Top.

It also can be argued that dust or pollen or moisture droplets created the orbs in grandson Connor's photographs (there was no rain), even though these orbs appeared at the Alabama Monument only while the music played and I read the names. Too, it is within the realm of chance that similar dust or pollen or moisture particles appeared only for an instant on Little Round Top and vanished in an instant, and also seemed to indicate movement. Also, it could be coincidence that an unexplained colorful mist appeared instantly after the orbs, and at the spot their apparent trajectory of travel was heading.

The fact that this all occurred where my own family members fought at Gettysburg, unbeknownst to me at the time, on a spot that has fascinated me for most of my life, also could be chalked up to coincidence.

After odds defying odds defy even more odds, however, I just can't write this all off as simple coincidence. That typing chimp certainly seems to be working overtime in this case.

I know the mind tends to stretch the facts to make sense of our world, and I recognize I am no exception to this, but there comes a point when chance seems to be influenced by a synergy in the universe.

Chapter 12

In My Mind's Eye

In July of 2017 I visited Gettysburg, accompanied by my friend Bruce Zigler, to sign books at the Gettysburg Paranormal Gathering at the David Stewart Farm.

By this time I had purchased a spirit box of my own, and when I had some free time during the trip we tried it out near the Alabama Monument. At first I received nothing through the device. But when I took the spirit box into the field east of the monument, asking repeatedly "Is anyone here with me?" at one point I received the answer "Yes."

To my query "Can you tell me your name?" I received the electronic voice reply "Tim." I could not make out any words through the static after that point, including when I asked for a full name.

When I returned to the Alabama Monument I again had no luck with the box. Bruce and I talked about what might elicit a response. Bruce noted that the Alabamians had a long march before moving against Little Round Top, so they may have wanted food. He asked "Are you hungry?" and received the clear reply, "I'm starving." Our further questioning yielded nothing more.

The apparent responses I received from the spirit box in the field were both one word, so I cannot rule out that they were quick blips from radio stations. My mindset here was one of looking for replies, so even though I was keenly aware of the possibility of radio blips, I have to be skeptical here. But the "I'm starving" response Bruce elicited did not sound remotely to me like radio blips were involved.

We then drove to Little Round Top, where efforts with the spirit box were fruitless. As I walked along the park road at the base of the 20th Maine's position on Little Round Top, however, I sensed a strange energy. Interestingly, this was the same feeling I encounter in my house just before or during unexplained events, such as disembodied footsteps or electronic devices malfunctioning. As I walked further, the energy subsided, but if I returned to the spot the feeling returned.

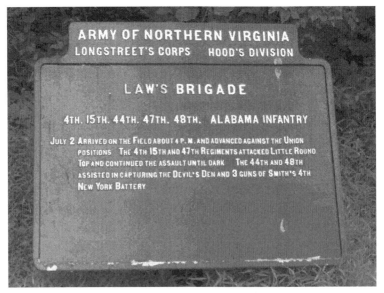

This is the marker for Law's Brigade that author Don Allison had not discovered before 2017. Author photo.

This energy "hotspot" was only about 10 or 15 feet wide. But as I walked up the slope it continued, until I reached the right of the 20th Maine battle line. And as I made my way back down the slope it continued, maintaining the same width but leading me back to and across the park road. I felt led through the boulder-strewn area there and then across the intersecting park drive. There I encountered a brass marker for Evander Law's Alabama Brigade I had not before seen. A look at an atlas for the battle indicated this marker was on the approach of the 15th Alabama in its attack against the Maine men.

Fast forward a few months to April 2018, following The Paranormal View crew weekend investigation at the Gettysburg Brew Works. I was again eager to visit Little Round Top. As it turned out, getting there was not so easy. The National Park Service had conducted a controlled burn in the area, so the roadways I typically use to reach the Round Tops were closed. I was determined to reach the area, however, and found a back way in.

There had been a persistent drizzle that day. Diane has been on Little Round Top many times, so she elected to remain in the van where she could stay dry while reading and listening to music. I didn't mind because at that point we were the only ones there, at the small parking area just south of the monument to the 20th Maine. I considered the rain and the road closings to be a blessing because I rarely have this area to myself.

Prior to our trip I had begun reading the book "Storming Little Round Top" by Phillip Thomas Tucker, detailing the experiences of the 15th Alabama at Gettysburg on July 2, 1863. Most of the reading I had done before obtaining this book had focused on the Union side of this fierce fight for the flank, so I was learning new details of the battle from the Southern perspective.

My goal had been to finish Tucker's book before leaving for Gettysburg, but I ran short of time and was only about midway through the narrative about the 15th's climactic struggle against the 20th Maine.

I left the van intending to climb the steps leading directly to the 20th Maine Monument, but appreciating that I was alone I stopped at the base of the hill. I felt inexplicably drawn to instead take a different route, so I began following the path that leads around the south end of the spur. I came up below a large boulder that I knew from previous visits was near the left flank marker of the 20th Maine at the crest of the ridge above me. In Tucker's book I had just read the account of the severe wounding of Lt. John Oates, younger brother of 15th Alabama commander Col. William Oates. The wounded Lt. Oates had been placed behind a large boulder to shield him from Federal fire and this certainly had to be the place. I reflected here for a few moments, then turned to head back toward the steps leading to the crest of the ridge.

Again, though, I felt drawn to turn around and continue on the path leading past the 20th Maine's left flank. As I walked slowly I continued to reflect, absorbing the atmosphere. I felt a calm but growing energy as I walked around the base of the ridge and then up the east side, heading toward the crest. I stopped to get my bearings, and to contemplate the energy I was sensing. It was a very peaceful feeling, actually calming despite the violent, bloody hand-to-hand fighting that I knew took place here.

I thought it odd that I had felt pulled to this point, as based on my understanding of the battle I was now beyond the left flank of the 20th Maine. Still I felt led to proceed toward the crest. As I reached the top of the ridge I suddenly could see in my mind's eye the area blanketed in swirling smoke, with the movement of arms and legs faintly visible through the thick haze. I could sense the yelling, the intensity, the muzzle blasts, the colliding soldiers.

Twice before this I had similar experiences at Civil War battlefields, once at Jonesboro, Georgia, and again at Gettysburg's East Cemetery Hill. Both were very tense experiences, draining almost all my energy and leaving me barely able to stand, let alone take a step. Both times the friends with me expressed concern, asking if I was OK.

This experience at Little Round Top, though, was less disturbing. As the smoky image slowly faded from my mind I stood motionless for several minutes, contemplating the experience. I felt like I was supposed to be here at this moment, that this is where my ancestors fought.

As I took stock of just where I was I realized something was wrong. I was standing at the crest of the ridge, facing west. The Alabamians never got this far, not to the crest. I tried moving back, then to the left, then to the right, but I only felt the energy at that same spot on the crest.

I felt, down to the deepest part of my being, that the Alabamians had reached this spot, as incorrect as I knew this to be.

It was not lost on me that I was standing at nearly the exact spot where psychic medium Tiffaney Mason had stopped and knelt a year earlier, facing west as I was facing now, the direction the Maine men should be facing, not the Alabamians. As she knelt here she had told me this was my family connection to Little Round Top. The fact that Tiffaney faced the wrong way nagged at me then, just as my position and orientation was bothering me now.

I felt an incredible sense of calm as I continued to stand there for several more minutes. Finally, as I felt the energy melting away, I headed back to the van and told Diane about my experience.

Back at the hotel that evening I pulled out my copy of "Storming Little Round Top" to read further into the progress of the battle.

Things certainly seemed to be falling into place when I read that my great-great-grandfather's company in the 15th Alabama, Company I, was among the companies ordered by Col. Oates to swing to the far right of the line in an attempt to outflank Col. Chamberlain and the 20th Maine.

I was astounded when I read Tucker's assertion that the Alabamians actually for a time carried the crest from behind, pushing the Maine men down the front of the hill.

I re-read that part of the book, feeling in awe as I thought back over my experience from that afternoon. Company I would have been right at the crest, right where I sensed the smoky, confused battle taking place, right where I felt that an unseen energy was directing me to be.

The memory of that moment of discovery is clearly etched in my mind, and I still feel the intensity when I think back on the experience.

Since returning home from that trip I've read and re-read various accounts of the 15th Alabama-20th Maine struggle, even studying maps drawn to the detail of each company's placement. This all reinforces the idea that somehow my intuition led me to the apex of my ancestor's advance during the battle.

As personally compelling as my experiences on Little Round Top may be, I certainly have not borne the burden of scientific proof regarding the validity of psychic perception. But the odds of this all coming together the way it did strictly by chance certainly seems implausible.

All the previous unusual camera malfunctions and photographic anomalies started me down this road. Tiffaney Mason's eerily accurate perceptions placing my family connection at the crest, a Southerner where a Northerner ought to be, are difficult to ignore.

Although I had found it strange, bordering on unbelievable, that Tiffaney referenced Joshua Chamberlain while we were together on Little Round Top, the fact that she mentioned the facts in controversy between

Oates and Chamberlain seems quite ironic in light of my own later experience at the crest.

As always, the questions are there. Did my experience with Tiffaney color my unconscious mind, and lead me to believe I felt an energy that led me to the crest? In effect, was it simply all in my mind?

Or is there more to it, that I indeed was tapping into an energy or communication with my ancestors? When my mind's eye is borne out by scholarship – facts that run counter to what I knew at the time – it certainly bolsters the argument that what happened is indeed real, even if we don't understand the mechanism behind it.

Were my ancestors somehow in fact telling their story, wanting me to know the truth? More so, as a writer, do I owe it to them to share this with the world?

Regardless of the cause, this was a very real experience for me, and I feel compelled to share it.

As I contemplate what this all means, I am coming to understand it was very much in the scheme of things that Tiffany spoke of Chamberlain while we were within the Little Round Top battle lines. I have read so much about Chamberlain, and think so highly of the man and his character, that he must have been in my mind at some level that day. Perhaps my thoughts sparked Tiffaney's perceptions.

With all this in mind I think of Chamberlain's own observation, the words of my ancestors' opponent himself. Beyond his service as a Union Army officer, Joshua Chamberlain was a college professor and theologian, and he wrote and spoke widely following the war. In yet another in this long string of spiritual connections, I realize that Chamberlain grappled with some of these very same thoughts. Speaking in Gettysburg on Oct. 3, 1889, during a ceremony dedicating Maine monuments there, Chamberlain famously observed:

In great deeds something abides. On great fields something stays. Forms change and pass; bodies disappear but spirits linger, to consecrate ground for the vision-place of souls.

And reverent men and women from afar, and generations that know us not and that we know not of, heart-drawn to see where and by whom great things were suffered and done for them, shall come to this deathless field, to ponder and dream; and lo! the shadow of a mighty presence shall wrap them in its bosom, and the power of the vision pass into their souls.

This Gettysburg National Battlefield Park marker describes the action at Little Round Top. Author photo.

Chapter 13

A Spirited Debate

So is Joshua Chamberlain right, do the spirits indeed still linger?

There certainly are indications – my own experiences, and the encounters of countless others – to give pause for thought that perhaps they do.

I have heard the argument that stories of ghosts on battlefields are disrespectful, desecrating what the soldiers fought for and sacrificed. Some people view the ghost tours, ghost books and ghost stories at Gettysburg in this light. I get that, and certainly want to pay all due respect to the soldiers and for that matter the civilians who were impacted. But consider the stories, books and movies that romanticize the war, that gloss over the loss and the gruesome bloodletting. Could those not be viewed in that same light?

It can be tempting for those of us interested in historic preservation and interpretation to put the past on a pedestal. But we need to be pragmatic. To keep the past alive we need to attract the attention of the public, and find a way to make it all financially feasible as well. A collection of artifacts may be well and good, but in today's world there has to be more. The draw may be hands-on immersion, or gift shop merchandise displays in windows to bring people into a historic building and perhaps entice them to pay for a tour. Even those ever-present felt kepis, plastic soldiers and toy muskets that fire caps can capture a child's imagination. If conducting ghost tours and selling books or videos on Gettysburg's paranormal connection draws the public's attention and enhances their knowledge of our history, I believe we should understand and appreciate that.

But close-mindedness where the paranormal is involved persists. I know full well, because I once held that same view. Now, though, I realize this is akin to those thought leaders centuries ago who clung to the old theory that the world was flat, and that was that.

A good example is the National Park Service, which has a policy at the Gettysburg Visitors Center against the sale of books on the paranormal. In 2015 I approached the company that handles their gift shop book sales about offering "I Met a Ghost at Gettysburg," and was told in no uncertain terms that the park service does not allow books on the paranormal. A couple who wanted to attend a September 2018 book signing of mine at the Gettysburg Heritage Center mistakenly went to the National Battlefield Park Visitors Center and were told I was not there, and it was made clear the park service does not sell books on the paranormal.

No less than the American Battlefield Trust, in an article on its website regarding seven myths at Gettysburg, takes a poke at Gettysburg ghosts.

Before I go on I will stress that I greatly respect and am a firm supporter of the American Battlefield Trust. Their amazing accomplishments in preserving and interpreting Civil War sites should receive a standing ovation from every American. I personally have been a member and supporter of the organization since it was known as the Association for the Preservation of Civil War Sites, and I encourage everyone to support the American Battlefield Trust and its mission.

However, I do take issue with the Trust's approach to the issue of ghosts. In its website article on myths at Gettysburg, the Trust directly states it is a myth that Gettysburg ghost stories are true. I agree that many such stories, most likely a great majority of them, are not true. But how can the writer of this statement conclude that *all* of them are fiction? In debunking any other myth of Gettysburg the author or authors certainly compile convincing evidence. So what is the evidence here? "With the exception of one story about Iverson's Pits near Oak Hill there were no substantially disseminated ghost stories at Gettysburg for more than a century," the article proclaims. "The ghosts at Gettysburg phenomenon started in the 1990s which happens to coincide with people starting to make money on ghost books and tours. Today, there are scores of books and tours available for visitors but most all of these stories are not historical in nature. The Civil War Trust's historian once heard a ghost story told in 1993. It was presented as fiction, but it only took three months until it was in a book as fact."

I don't dispute the claim about the historian hearing a fictional story later passed off as true, or that many of the ghost stories are not based in documented facts. Anyone who has ever researched history and compared it to the commercialization of historic sites realizes that does happen, and happens often. But it stands to reason that citing one particular error does not indict an entire proposition.

Beyond that, I also take issue with the rather simplistic dismissal of ghost stories beyond the account of Iverson's pits, by claiming there were no "substantially disseminated" ghost stories at Gettysburg for more than a century. The word substantially is of course subjective, not objective. Dissemination of information was much slower and much more difficult in the 1800s and early 1900s than today. Digital printing, social media and electronic channels of communication certainly make dissemination of stories faster now, wider and more pervasive than in decades past. Not just ghost stories, but pretty much everything began being more substantially disseminated with the growth of the internet in the 1990s, and the subsequent explosion of social media.

Were there ghost stories from the Gettysburg area in the years just after the epic battle? Of course there were, and they were disseminated.

Some of Gettysburg's ghost stories predate the Civil War. In fact, legends link Gettysburg's ghostly reputation to the area's Native Americans. In its Aug. 27, 1833 issue, the Gettysburg Compiler recounts the story of a ghost that allegedly led a group of men in Gettysburg to dig in an unsuccessful search for buried treasure. Ironically, the Compiler report served as fodder for debate over the then-current movement against the Masonic order.

In her 1972 book "Haunts of Adams County and Other Counties," Sally Barach details a number of regional ghost stories, many dating to the 1700s. Two relate to the Revolutionary War and vanquished Hessian soldiers. Barach writes that Hessians captured during the

Battle of Trenton were being taken by horse and sled to Frederick, Maryland, and that Gettysburg was a stop on the way. The story claims that the Hessians were lodged overnight in a Gettysburg tavern – its exact location has been lost through time – and that their guards became drunk. The guards did not want the responsibility of the prisoners, the story claims, so they stabbed the Hessians to death. Subsequently, Barach writes, "Legend has it that the tavern was fearfully haunted. Shrieks and cries, pleas for mercy and howls of agony were reported to issue from its upstairs rooms."

Barach relates a second story involving these same Hessians taken captive in 1788. Stating the source was a newspaper account from more than a century ago – that is, before 1872, based on the 1972 vintage of Barach's book – she writes that a couple in a sleigh were approaching a covered bridge over Conewago Creek, about halfway between Littlestown, Pennsylvania, and Hanover, Maryland, on a dark and snowy night. According to this account the couple's horses became frightened and refused to cross the bridge. "To the astonishment of the couple in the sleigh," Barach writes, "there passed alongside them another sleigh of long, low frame and ancient vintage. Seated in the sleigh other than the driver were about a dozen uniformed men, arranged in two rows and facing each other. The men and sleigh passed by silently, there was not even the sound of the horses that pulled them. Later the couple checked the uniforms which they had noted on the men, and found them to be those of the Hessian Army, of Revolutionary War times."

Yet another story, shared by Troy Taylor, originates soon after the Gettysburg battle. Taylor states the widow of Confederate Brigadier Gen. William Barksdale, a casualty of the conflict, traveled to Gettysburg to have his body removed for reburial in Mississippi. (By some accounts the body was exhumed more than three years after the battle.) This story claims that she brought along her husband's favorite hunting dog. "As the old dog was led to his master's grave," Taylor wrote, "he fell down on the ground and began to howl. No matter what Mrs. Barksdale did, she was unable to pull the animal away."

Taylor noted the dog watched over the grave throughout the night and the next day, refusing Mrs. Barksdale's efforts to lure it away even though the general's body had been removed. "Finally, saddened by the dog's pitiful loyalty, she left for home," he wrote.

According to Taylor, the dog remained at the grave, refusing food and occasionally letting out a mournful howl, and eventually died from hunger and thirst. "Within a few years," he continued, "a tale began to circulate that the animal's spirit still lingered at the Hummelbaugh Farm.

It has been said that on the night of July 2, the anniversary of Barksdale's death, an unearthly howl echoes into the night ... as the faithful hunting dog still grieves from a place beyond this world."

And then there is an account involving Gettysburg's civilian hero, John Burns. Although 70 years old at the time of the battle the grizzled War of 1812 veteran grabbed his flintlock musket and joined the Union troops for the first day's fight. He sustained several wounds, but survived the fray.

The grave of War of 1812 veteran John Burns, who as a civilian shouldered his flintlock musket to join the Union troops in the July 1, 1863 fighting at Gettysburg. He has wounded but recovered. He died in 1872 and is buried in Gettysburg's Evergreen Cemetery. Author photo.

In the 1875 book "Martial Deeds of Pennsylvania," Samuel Bates relates this account of an 1866 interview with Burns:

"He was never quite satisfied with the fight at Gettysburg, especially on that first day, when the Union forces were obliged to yield their position. He never mentioned the subject without expressing the wish that the rebels would come once more, believing that if the battle was to be fought over again he could do better. He manifested great reluctance to speak of his wounds, and only after repeated importunities could he be induced to show his scars, which disclose how horrible must have been his mutilation ...

"With all his heroism, Burns was not without a spark of superstition. It may have been a relic of family or national tradition, or a constitutional trace of morbid religious sentiment with which he was thoroughly imbued. He believed in apparitions. He was on one occasion passing through the woods, where in the battle he had fought. It was summer, and the foliage was upon the forest as then.

"He was alone, no human being within call, when suddenly there appeared before him a Confederate soldier, dressed in gray, with slouched hat, gun and accouterments. 'He was,' says Burns, 'a man of immense proportions and the very image of the one whom I had seen there on the day of the battle, at the very spot, and in the exact attitude.'

"'Did you speak to it?' we asked. 'No, sir, I did not. It beckoned me to come towards him, but I turned and left the ground as rapidly as I could, and have never been on that field since. I could face them alive and respond to their challenge, but when the dead men come back, I am not in for that style of warfare.'

"'But Mr. Burns, you do not really believe that it was a ghost, do you?'

"Shaking his head as if still in awe of the apparition, and with solomn and mysterious mien, he exclaimed, 'Ah, Ha! You tell if you can.'"

Of course I have encountered even more such stories, but I think I have sufficiently made my point. I certainly am not vouching for the truth or accuracy of these accounts, although they typical of paranormal accounts through the ages. I am just proving such stories do indeed exist, and obviously were disseminated well before the 1990s.

Another factor here – and it strikes to the core of why I have stressed this argument so forcefully – is the fear that people held and still hold about being judged for sharing a paranormal encounter. Today discussion of the paranormal is becoming more widely accepted. That, however, has not always been the case. Consider the fear people had in the 1800s of being judged should they share their paranormal encounters, and how they would have most often kept their experiences to themselves. Even people my own age have told me they kept their childhood paranormal encounters to themselves for fear of being accused of having hallucinations, or of having their sanity questioned.

The key to understanding any topic is encouraging healthy debate – do the research and support your position, don't simply dismiss without evidence that with which you disagree.

The American Battlefield Trust article proclaiming ghost stories to be a myth concludes with, "By all means, believe what you want to believe but please know that if water gets on a camera lens, it's water — not a ghostly 'orb.' If sun shines into a camera lens, it's called sunlight, not an 'energy sphere.'"

Yes, there are people willing to claim that a photograph of a shadow, a reflection in a window or a camera flash reflecting off a speck of dust is evidence of the paranormal. But there also are intriguing photos that defy easy explanation, including orbs, which deserve further consideration and study. To be close-minded and dismissive serves no one's best interest.

Again I want to stress that I make this argument not to bash the American Battlefield Trust, but to make a point. I cannot say enough that the organization has done, is doing, and in the future will continue to do great things in preserving and interpreting our heritage. I remain a staunch supporter of the group and its mission. Rather, I believe that to advance scientific knowledge and our understanding of the world, we have to be open to finding the answers to any and all questions.

If the board wants to state that its members do not believe in the existence of ghosts at Gettysburg, I respect that. In the Trusts' own words, "By all means, believe what you want to believe ..." But as a serious, inquisitive journalist I have written this book and one other imploring us to be open to the possibility of forces of nature we do not understand. If someone researching a trip to Gettysburg takes the American Battlefield Trust statement at face value, they may well see my book, believe it is mythology and pass it by.

I would argue against anyone blindly dismissing all paranormal accounts out of hand. I believe what I have presented in this book and "I Met a Ghost at Gettysburg" is worth consideration. I am far from alone in my assertions. As a trained, experienced professional photographer, I caution against writing off all orbs as water or sunlight, especially when they occur in conjunction with other paranormal evidence.

Mankind progresses in knowledge and understanding by asking questions, as potentially controversial as they may be, and trying our best to find the answers using valid methods of inquiry.

In my opinion, the only truly stupid question is one that is never asked.

This photo is an example of judgment calls that come into play when evaluating possible paranormal evidence. The well is near the Gettysburg Brew Works, a field hospital for Confederates wounded in the Culp's Hill area. As a series of photos was taken author Don Allison asked if anyone was with the group and named off Confederate states. The orb at upper left appeared immediately after he called out South Carolina. No orbs appeared in the other photos. Although South Carolina troops fought at Culp's Hill, the author would not include this photo except for another piece of evidence. About a minute earlier, a digital recorder picked up the answer "I am" to an investigator's query of "Is anybody with us?" The orb is intriguing, but is it simply dust and coincidence? Courtesy of Logan Smallwood.

Chapter 14

Final Thoughts

Unlike my mindset when I finished "I Met a Ghost at Gettysburg," I am not through addressing the paranormal. I plan to continue my work as a historian as well, to be sure, but my quest for knowledge about unexplained phenomenon is not over.

From my own experience and research as well as from talking with many others, I've found that personal experience is typically the key to belief, or disbelief, in the reality of paranormal events. In that light, I see potential in public ghost hunts conducted by credible groups. For a fee, people can be taken to a reportedly haunted location, assisted with investigative techniques and equipment, and perhaps have a real life paranormal encounter. This can be life changing. I know. Look no further than Connor and me, and our ghost box concert and conversation with the apparent Ohio captain. If you never have had a personal paranormal encounter, I recommend you consider going the public investigation route.

If you haven't had a paranormal encounter of your own, perhaps this book is the next best thing. I realize nothing I have presented here is scientific proof of the paranormal. No one yet has ever presented such proof. But the experiences I have shared here are conclusive evidence *to me*.

I have had many, many more experiences that may have been paranormal than I have presented here. What I have attempted to do is be selective, to only present instances where several parts of the experience line up, such as visual evidence, dowsing rod results and the historical record providing a match, or a psychic's findings being separately corroborated. I have tried to build a case as best I can that we all should take this seriously.

In my opinion paranormal investigators can play a role in collecting evidence to help advance the field. Currently, though, I see many shortcomings. One problem is that anyone can become an investigator. No formal training is required, there are no guidelines investigators must adhere to. Often television shows provide the basic instruction. The fact that investigators frequently fail to follow scientific protocols, and are quick to point to a single orb or reflection or shadow or unexplained garble on an audio recorder as evidence of the paranormal, too often subjects the entire field to suspicion if not ridicule, such as the Gettysburg myths article.

And don't take local legends or word of mouth stories at face value. If a murder supposedly took place at a location, be sure it actually happened. Go the local library and research history books and old newspaper accounts, and go to the courthouse to see the court records. If so-and-so supposedly owned the house and died there, check out old real estate and death records. Don't be afraid to ask local historians, librarians or government clerks to assist you. Most often they will.

If you are investigating simply in search of a personal experience, that is fine. But if you are trying to collect evidence to further the study of the paranormal, then you should learn and follow proper scientific and documentation protocol.

It can be easy to fall prey to the urge to claim you have found evidence when in fact that conclusion is simply not justified. I can share a recent temptation of my own. During an August 2018 visit to the Slyder House at Gettysburg, the field hospital for the Alabama Brigade after the Little Round Top fight, while on my way back to my van along the walking path I heard what sounded very much like large caliber muskets firing in the distance. Moments later I heard the distinct boom of a cannon. I knew there was an artillery demonstration on the battlefield that day, so I immediately drove over to check it out. However, to my surprise, the reenactors had finished for the day and were gone.

Someone wanting evidence of the paranormal may be tempted to cite this as an example of the mysterious sounds of weapons so frequently reported at Gettysburg. That would be too much of a stretch, however. It is quite likely there was a living history demonstration going on somewhere nearby of which I was not aware, and lacking other evidence I must conclude that reenactors were the most likely source of the sounds.

So what can be done to advance the field of paranormal studies, and the scientific validation of evidence the investigators uncover?

At this point I believe parapsychology holds the best answers, as this field can draw from various disciplines in the quest for knowledge. During The Paranormal View's April 2017 investigation at the Fairfield Inn I met Darcie McGrath, an experienced paranormal investigator who teaches parapsychology courses at the college level. She trained under Loyd Auerbach, whose works in paranormal investigation I have found to be enlightening.

On Sept. 19, 2018, I spoke with Darcie by telephone to explore her thoughts on parapsychology, which basically studies the relationship between the human mind and its environment.

"That's what parapsychology is, the study of human consciousness," Darcie explained. "They call it psi."

What led Darcie, a technology communicator who works in engineering, to become a parapsychologist? "I actually started when I was a kid," she said. "I remember telling a librarian 'There's no such thing as ghosts.' I was maybe 8 at the time. So she took me to the nonfiction section." There, Darcie said, she found the book "Haunted Houses" by Larry Kettelkamp. "I got my first experience through that book, as to what all this stuff is."

In addition to her nearly lifelong interest in paranormal research, Darcie also describes herself as a sensitive – in a nutshell someone who is able to pick up on vibes that others usually miss, including a degree of psychic abilities.

I proposed to Darcie my theory that being exposed to frequent paranormal experiences in my home has given me a heightened sense of the energies that accompany hauntings. Darcie said she agreed that is possible. "Your senses just get attuned when you live in a haunted location," she said.

Darcie also was quick to agree that lack of proper research of the historic record hinders acceptance of paranormal investigators' findings, especially at places where a reported haunting represents a chance for profits. "I think truth is one of the first casualties of paranormal commerce," she said, "the tendency to dramaticize things, or stretch the truth, or go by hearsay."

I asked Darcie how paranormal investigators can improve their craft, to properly follow the scientific method and present a better case to skeptics. "The Rhine Research Center has always been my go-to, as far as understanding the scientific method," she replied.

In essence the scientific method involves recognizing a problem, collecting data through observation and experiment, and forming and testing hypotheses.

According to Darcie, following the scientific method includes knowing how to properly use investigative equipment, such as doing a baseline scan before collecting electromagnetic field evidence. She said it also involves "being able to understand, of course, what a ghost is – we don't know." An EMF meter is able to detect electromagnetic fields, "but that doesn't mean it's a ghost," she said. "It's important to know what your device is doing, and how it works."

By not approaching paranormal investigation in a scientific manner, she said, "It makes it very difficult for scientists to take what investigators are doing very seriously." It boils down to quantitative and qualitative thinking, she explained. "Having something happen on one investigation is not a scientific finding," she said. "It's important to know how to make a scientific study.

They have to understand that they have to share, and be subject to peer review. You are building a case and that's a thing a lot of people in the paranormal field tend to miss."

"There is a schism – a chasm – between parapsychologists and investigators," she said. Paranormal investigators believe parapsychology academics are too stuffy, she said, and parapsychologists say investigators are not being scientific enough.

"I think that chasm can be filled with a little more training by the paranormal investigators," she continued. "But they have to want to do it." She recommended the Rhine Research Center as a good place to begin, and said she was planning to offer parapsychology for investigators as an online course.

As a final question for Darcie, I asked her opinion on advances being made in quantum physics. "That's going to blow everything wide open," she replied. "It just has to be applied the right way." She believes it will be difficult to find a tenured researcher willing to take the chance in this field, and it may be up to "weekend warriors" to take up the challenge. "I'm really excited to see where this is going to go."

"Psi activity is not a super power," Darcie said, "it's normal."

I definitely agree with Darcie. Although paranormal events cannot be accounted for with our current scientific knowledge, I believe further research can tell us more. As for paranormal investigators, I hope many will indeed take Darcie's advice and pursue training, and strictly follow the scientific method. I also hope they will continue to offer members of the public the chance to take part in an investigation, to experience a paranormal encounter themselves.

It is my sincere hope that the skeptics among my readers will keep an open mind. There is a great unexplored world out there. By being open and inquisitive, perhaps they will catch a glimpse into that world, as I and countless others have done.

One saying I've encountered is "The plural of anecdote is not evidence." Within the guidelines of the scientific method, that is correct. However, when countless people through recorded history have mysterious experiences that share many similarities, if it's not evidence then at least it's something we doggone well ought to be paying attention to. Be skeptical, yes, but I believe we all must keep an open mind.

And perhaps more than anything, I hope a young person pursuing a career in quantum physics runs across this book and is intrigued. If you are reading this and you know such a person, please pass on this book to him or her, or at least point the individual in my direction.

If I accomplish nothing else in my life from here on out, if I can help motivate a talented scientist to strive to find the breakthrough, the groundbreaking methods that will uncover answers to this myriad of mysteries, then I will consider this work a success.

So if you fit the above description, I encourage you to take up the challenge: Give us answers that will convert the paranormal to the normal.

About the Author

Don Allison, a veteran journalist and author, is a lifelong resident of Williams County, Ohio, where he shares a historic home with his wife, Diane. A 1976 graduate of Stryker High School, Don earned a bachelor of arts degree in journalism from the University of Toledo in 1980.

As a high school student Don got his start in journalism as a sports writer and photographer with the weekly Advance Reporter newspaper, now known as the Village Reporter. He joined The Bryan Times in 1981, where he served many years as news editor and currently is semi-retired and is senior editor. He has received numerous Associated Press and United Press International awards for his news, feature and column writing and special section design. Don's weekly column "On My Mind" is a Bryan Times fixture.

Drawing on knowledge gained from a lifetime of studying the Civil War, Don has written extensively about that conflict. He and Diane are the founders of Faded Banner Publications, which publishes books on the Civil War and Northwest Ohio history, as well as the paranormal.

Currently Don is co-authoring, with fellow Northwest Ohio historian Richard Cooley, a book on the 38th Ohio Volunteer Infantry in the Civil War.

For nearly four decades Don has served on the Williams County, Ohio, Historical Society Board of Trustees, and through the years he has held various offices with the organization. He spearheaded the successful effort in which the society acquired and preserved the 1845 Society of Friends Meeting House in western Williams County. Don also is a founding member and past trustee and officer of the Stryker Area Heritage Council. Currently Don serves as an interpreter with the Sauder Village, Archbold, Ohio.

Don's previous books include "I Met a Ghost at Gettysburg: A Journalist's Journey Into the Paranormal," "Hell on Belle Isle: Diary of a Civil War POW" and "The Best of On My Mind: The Bryan Times Newspaper Columns of Don Allison." Each is available for $16.95 plus $3.50 shipping and handling from Faded Banner Publications, PO Box 101, Bryan, OH 43506. In addition, copies may be ordered online at www.fadedbanner.com.

Sources

The three crew members from the Gettysburg area who served together on the B-17 Mason and Dixon during World War II were featured in an article in the Gettysburg Times on Nov. 11, 1996. Further information on the Mason and Dixon and its crew is available at https://100thbg.com.

Information on Hans Holzer is based on his obituary in the New York Times on April 29, 2009, at www.britannica.com and as well as material in his book "Ghosts: True Encounters With the World Beyond" (Black Dog & Leventhal Publishers Inc., 2004).

Loyd Auebach's information was taken from "Ghost Hunting: How to Investigate the Paranormal" (Ronin Publishing Inc., Oakland, California 2004) and his biographical information listed at www.parapsych.org.

The segment on journalist Michael Clarkson's writing in the paranormal field is based on information contained in Alexandra Holzer's Sept. 18, 2012 piece in The Huffington Post. Interestingly, Holzer is the daughter of Hans Holzer.

Rod Steiger's biographical information is taken from the opening pages of his book "Real Ghosts, Restless Spirits, and Haunted Places" (Visible Ink Press, Canton, Michigan, 2003).

Background information on Mark Nesbitt is based on Don and Diane Allison's interview with Nesbitt on Oct.

12, 2009, and subsequent email and telephone conversations between Don and Mark.

Biographical information on Robert Dale Owen was drawn from www.wikipedia.org, www.britannica.com, www.biography.com and bioguide.congress.gov.

Michael Brooks, writing in New Scientist of July 19, 2009, offers a scientific explanation of how dowsing rods work. See also a Feb. 24, 2009 article by Sarah Zielinski at Smithsonian.com, and a Nov. 22, 2017 piece by Philip Ball at www.theguardian.com. However, at www.groundwateruk.org, the UK Groundwater Forum concludes that in some cases people can locate buried pipes with rods or twigs. And the November 1998 edition of Popular Mechanics, also posted online at www.popularmechanics.com on Dec. 6, 2004, reports statistically significant results in finding water using dowsing rods, attributing human sensitivity to electromagnetic energy as the cause.

Information on field hospitals near Sachs Covered Bridge was taken from Page 49 of "Gettysburg Civil War Field Hospital Tour," sponsored by Historic Gettysburg-Adams County and The Hospital & Health System Association of Pennsylvania, July 2001. The information on the union hospital at the Michael Trostle Farm on Sachs Road is on page 20 of this work.

The American Society of Dowsers website is https://dowsers.org. Information on dowsing was drawn from this site, and from an article by Jason Blevins in the Denver Post that first appeared June 5, 2009, and updated May 6, 2016. "Cecil Downing and Gettysburg's Triangular Field" by Joe Farrell appears in

The American Dowser Quarterly Digest, Vol. 37, No, 3, Summer 1997, pages 66-72.

Albert Einstein's quote regarding dowsing was taken from a Feb. 15, 1946, letter to Herman E. Peisach. This quote was taken from http://archive.li and is referenced in a number of other sources.

The explanation of the double slit experiment and its implications is taken from Pages 31 and 32 of "Quantum Parapsychology: How Science is Proving the Paranormal" by David Jacobs and Sarah Soderlund (JS Books, 2017); Popular Mechanics, "The Logic-Defying Double Slit Experiment is Even Weirder Than You Thought," Aug. 11, 2016, by Avery Thompson; The Scientific American, "What Does the New Double Slit Experiment Actually Show," June 7, 2011, by Matthew Francis; www.physicsworld.com, "Do Atoms Going Through a Double Slit 'Know' They are Being Observed?", May 26, 2015.

The description of parapsychology is taken from information provided by the Rhine Research Center, www.rhine.org; the Parapsychological Association, www.parapsych.org; and from Psychology Today, www.psychologytoday.com.

Benjamin Radford is the author of "Scientific Paranormal Investigation: How to Solve Unexplained Mysteries" (Rhombus Publishing Company, 2010). Information on Radford's background was taken from this book, and his article "Are Ghosts Real – Information Has Not Materialized," dated May 17, 2017, in Live Science. The telephone interview with Radford took place following the publication of "I Met a Ghost at Gettysburg."

Historical information on the Fairview Inn came from the inn's website at http://thefairfieldinn.com. The description of wagon trains carrying the wounded came from numerous passages of the book "Retreat from Gettysburg: Lee, Logistics and the Pennsylvania Campaign" by Kent Masterson Brown (The University of North Carolina Press, 2005), especially Pages 106-124.

Accounts of wounded cavalrymen being cared for in Fairfield following the nearby July 3, 1863 cavalry fight were taken from various sources, including Fairfield Historical District documentation.

Information on the Jarvis, Champion and Goodwin men's service in Alabama units came from numerous archive and other sources, including several that were accessed through anecestor.com; The Civil War Soldiers and Sailors System database; as well as the website https://www.algw.org/henry/military/15thal.htm.

Overall information on the Little Round Top fight between the 20th Maine and 15th Alabama was taken from the article "Movements Of Companies Of the 20th Maine and 15th Alabama Regiments During the Attack On Little Round Top" by Lowell Getz that is found at www.ideals.illinois.edu; "The Twentieth Maine" by John J. Pullen, 1957; "Storming Little Round Top" by Phillip Thomas Tucker (Da Capo Press, 2002); "The Fighting Fifteenth Alabama Infantry: A Civil War History and Roster" by James P. Faust (McFarland & Company Inc., Jefferson, N.C., 2014), Chapter 5; and "Stand Firm Ye Boys from Maine: The 20th Maine and the Gettysburg Campaign, Fifteenth Anniversary Edition" by Thomas A. Desjardin (Oxford University Press, Oxford, New York, 2009).

The Alabama Brigade's involvement and movements at Gettysburg are detailed in "Struggle for the Round Tops: Law's Alabama Brigade at the Battle of Gettysburg" by Morris M. Penney and J. Gary Laine (Burd Street Press, Division of White Mane Publishing Company Inc., Shippensburg, Pennsylvania, 1999). Also consulted for information on the Alabama Brigade was "Law's Alabama Brigade in the War Between the Union and the Confederacy" by J. Gary Laine and Morris M. Penney (White Mane Publishing Company Inc., Shippensburg, Pennsylvania, 1996), particularly Pages 66 to 126.

Joshua Chamberlain's quote at the Maine Monument dedication on Oct. 3, 1889, in Gettysburg was taken from www.joshuachamberlain.com.

Seven myths at Gettysburg by The American Battlefield Trust: https://www.battlefields.org/learn/articles/7-gettysburg-myths-and-misconceptions.

Troy Taylor's account of Confederate Brigadier Gen. William Barksdale's dog refusing to leave the general's gravesite on the field at Gettysburg is drawn from the article "America's Most Haunted Places: A Road Trip Into the Supernatural, Gettysburg Battlefield," at http://www.prairieghosts.com/gettysburg.html.

"Haunts of Adams County and Other Counties" by Sally Barach (A.G. Halldin Publishing Company, Indiana, Pennsylvania, 1972) contains 46 pages detailing stories of hauntings in Gettysburg, Adams County and the surrounding region.

The account of John Burns' encounter with a ghost was shared with Don Allison by Timothy H. Smith, author of "John Burns: The Hero of Gettysburg" (Thomas Publications, 2000). The original citation is contained on Page 996 of "Martial Deeds of Pennsylvania" by Samuel Bates (T.H. Davis & Co, Philadelphia, 1875).

Some of the information on theories regarding paranormal occurrences and ghost hunting techniques came from "The Ghost Hunters Field Guide: Gettysburg and Beyond," by Mark Nesbitt (Second Chance Publications, Gettysburg, Pa., 2005), Pages 8 to 45; and "Ghost Hunting: How to Investigate the Paranormal" by Loyd Auerbach (Ronin Publishing Inc., Oakland, California 2004).

The approximate number of troops engaged at Gettysburg and casualty figures cited are based on a survey of modern sources, in which the totals vary by insignificant amounts.

Index

Made in the USA
Middletown, DE
31 October 2020

22990035R00075